Tales
from the
ADIRONDACK
FOOTHILLS
by
HOWARD THOMAS

Sketches by John Mahaff

NORTH COUNTRY BOOKS, INC.
Utica, New York

TALES OF THE ADIRONDACK FOOTHILLS

Prospect Books 1980
First Paperback Printing 2002

ISBN 0-925168-41-6

NORTH COUNTRY BOOKS, INC.
311 Turner Street
Utica, New York 13501

FOREWORD

It is with great pleasure that North Country Books is able to reprint this book. The late Bill Thomas, former owner of Prospect Books, was a good friend to me personally as well as to North Country Books and to all lovers of the Adirondacks.

Bill took great pride in keeping books available that he felt told yet another bit of the Adirondack history and lore, which he loved so much. Some years ago when he was ready to retire from the business of publishing, he entrusted the legacy of Prospect Books to North Country Books. Bill was pleased that he had found what he felt to be a good home for his books. I hope you agree.

As with many of the books that North Country Books reprints, Tales from the Adirondack Foothills is being reprinted in its original form, with only minor changes where absolutely necessary.

SHEILA ORLIN
Publisher

FOREWORD

The Adirondack foothills climb abruptly north of the Mohawk Valley from Amsterdam on the east to Rome on the west. A peak might rise occasionally to 2000 feet above sea level, but for the most part the hills are gentle and rolling, with little of the cragginess which characterizes the Adirondack Mountains to the north.

Over the past century and a half, much of the virgin timber has been cut from the foothills to provide lumber for building, fuel for stoves and fireplaces, and pulp for paper. Reforestation has in many instances brought new growths of pine, fir and hemlock.

The chief industry in the Adirondack foothills has always been dairying, for the pioneers who cleared the wilderness realized that the rocky hill country, with its inferior fertility, could not compete with the low lands of the Mohawk and St. Lawrence river valleys in the raising of ground crops. Butter and cheese became the chief products of the area, and the sale of milk to the cities has now replaced both as the major industry.

The virgin forest provided a seemingly endless supply of timber and for many years logs were driven down the East Canada and West Canada Creeks and the Black and Moose Rivers. Dolgeville, Hinckley, Forestport and Lyons Falls became important centers for the lumbering interests, and picturesque lumberjacks riding white water were familiar and thrilling sights along these streams.

Small settlements predominate in the Adirondack foothills. There are no cities between Utica and Watertown and few large villages. Probably the average population of a foothills village is 500 people. A half century ago, these villages were self-sufficient, but with the coming of mechanized industry, they found themselves dependent on the cities and large villages for employment and for many of the necessities of life.

They have not, however, relinquished their spirit of independence, a characteristic of all hill people, and they each possess a sense of local pride which finds vent in community projects which are often more extensively carried on than by the citizens of the cities.

Wars have merely brushed the skirts of the Adirondack foothills and their people have seldom been thrown into the thick of political affairs. For the most part, they have lived a quiet, stable life based on the home, the school, the church and the community.

This seeming lack of prominence has often led to the assumption that they have played a merely passive part in the life of the nation. Nothing could be farther from the truth. Men prominent in national affairs have lived and died in the area. Industries vital to the nation have thrived and still strive here. And the people themselves have made a mass contribution to good citizenship which is noteworthy in a nation often criticized as being careless of its birthright of freedom.

In these tales of the Adirondack foothills, the author has tried to bring together a collection of stories, biographies and anecdotes which he hopes give a better picture of the hill country and its people. Many of these stories have appeared before, in county histories, in newspapers and in books written about the region. Some of them are word-of-mouth tales which have never before seen the light of print. It is his hope that the reader will not only find them entertaining but that they will give him a better understanding of the section of America in which he lives.

HOWARD THOMAS

CONTENTS

CONTENTS

TALES
from the
ADIRONDACK FOOTHILLS

PART I

WARS AND INDIANS

PISKARET

Centuries ago, when America was young and the only humans to wander through the great North Woods were Indians, a feud to the death arose between the Algonquins and the Iroquois. The latter, being the stronger and the more warlike, drove their enemies out of the woods into Canada, where the Algonquins made a last ditch stand at Three Rivers.

When the French came to Canada, the Algonquins saw an opportunity to revenge themselves on the Iroquois. They swooped down on their enemies and murdered some promising young braves. The Iroquois, in retaliation, went forth in small parties of guerillas and set out to exterminate the Algonquins, village by village. The latter, having been driven as far as Quebec, decided to counter with similar methods.

According to Adirondack folklore, the most famous guerilla leader of the Algonquins was a chief named Piskaret. Together with four companions, he set out from Three Rivers in a single canoe. Each brave had three muskets, each double-loaded. They had not gone far up the Sorel River when they ran into a party of 50 Iroquois braves, all decked out for the warpath, paddling along in five birchbark canoes. The Algonquins resorted to deception. Pretending to be overwhelmed by this superior force, they began to howl their death song. The Iroquois, usually the craftiest of Indians, paddled in for the kill.

Piskaret and his braves waited until the Iroquois were quite close; then they broke off their wailing and poured lead into their enemies. The Iroquois' canoes foundered and sank. Piskaret knocked the warriors over the head as they struggled in the water. He saved a few to torture before burning them alive.

This sudden extermination of 50 Iroquois braves encouraged the crafty Piskaret. He started out alone one spring, wearing his snowshoes backward to throw off his enemies. After penetrating deep into the Adirondacks, he came upon a small village. When night fell, he sneaked into one of the cabins while its inmates lay asleep and murdered all the occupants. He retired to the forest, his belt lined with bloody scalps.

The Iroquois, offended and angered by this sneak attack, sent out parties in search of the marauder, but Piskaret, carefully concealed near the village, sneered silently at their frantic but futile efforts to capture him. At midnight he again crept into the village, chose another cabin, and fled to the woods with more scalps.

After searching for him all the next day, the Iroquois retired for the night, but posted a sentinel to warn against attack. The bold Piskaret crept into the village and lifted the sentinel's scalp, but the latter set up such a howling that the whole village was aroused. Piskaret, the fastest runner in the Adirondacks, led them a merry chase. He would slow down, make his presence known with taunts and jeers, and then simply outrun his pursuers.

At nightfall he and his enemies were deep in the Adirondack wilderness. The Iroquois, thinking themselves in no danger of attack by a solitary brave, threw themselves on the ground and fell into a sleep of exhaustion.

Piskaret was wide awake. He turned back, took off his snowshoes and crawled on hands and knees into the Iroquois camp. The loud snoring of the braves told him what he wanted to know. He kept an eye peeled for a sentinel, but the careless Iroquois had neglected to post one.

The braves lay prone, wrapped in their blankets near a dying campfire. Piskaret sneaked up to one, knocked him over the head and lifted his scalp. Encouraged by success, he went through the camp, repeating the process. He performed with such skill that hardly a groan rose from the doomed men. After eliminating the whole party, he returned to Three Rivers with the largest collection of scalps ever worn by an Algonquin.

The Mohawks, who were the chief victims of Piskaret, blamed the French for this insult. They murdered Father Isaac Jogues and a young man named Lalande, flung their bodies into the Mohawk River and set their heads up on poles for all to see.

They also set out on the warpath against the Algonquins. After burning and plundering Fort Richelieu, a French outpost at the outlet of Lake Champlain, they ran into an Algonquin village which lay defenseless, its braves being out on a hunt. They captured the women and children and set fire to the cabins.

The Algonquin hunters, returning too late, were trapped by the Mohawks. Most of them were killed or captured. Piskaret, brave to the end, was dispatched by a sword thrust through his body.

BIG MOUTH AND THE RAT

When Samuel de Champlain drew his blunderbuss and killed several frightened Iroquois in May, 1609, he brought down upon the heads of the French the bitter enmity of the Iroquois nation. Over a century of warfare followed this first display of firearms in the northern wilderness. The Iroquois, French-haters to the last brave, eventually aided the British in driving the Fleur-de-lis out of the New World.

The French made repeated efforts to pacify their Indian enemies. In 1688 a band of 1200 Onondaga, Cayuga and Oneida warriors journeyed to Montreal to draw up a declaration of neutrality. Their leader, Garangula or Big Mouth, arrived like a haughty conqueror and declared that but for his influence all the French settlements would have been destroyed. He agreed to send delegates to a peace treaty and signed the neutrality pact with pictures of birds and animals. He refused to include the Canadian Indians in the agreement.

This act aroused the ire of a Huron chief named Kon-di-a-ronk or the Rat, who felt sure that the Iroquois would attack his people as soon as the treaty had been signed. He resolved to circumvent the Iroquois, so he set sail down Lake Ontario to Henderson Harbor to lie in wait for their emissaries.

The Iroquois delegation, led by a famous chief, Te-gan-i-so-rens, three minor chiefs and a few warriors, put in at Henderson Harbor to rest. The Rat, who had been waiting five days for his opportunity, fired into the Iroquois party, killing one chief and wounding several warriors. Rushing forth with his men, he took the whole party prisoners.

The Rat proved a good name for the Huron chief. He feigned innocence of the peace mission and declared that the French governor had told him to intercept the Iroquois party. He vowed that he would not be satisfied until the Five Nations wiped the French intruders off the map of America. He sent the surviving Iroquois back, carrying with them a supply of guns and ammunition and a deep hatred of the French.

The Rat kept one man prisoner and took him along to Fort Frontenac, where he remarked, "I have killed the peace. We shall now see how the governor will get out of this business." Without waiting for any comment from the French, he took himself off to Mackinaw, taking with him the Iroquois prisoner, whom he claimed he wished to adopt.

5

Once they were at Mackinaw, the Iroquois told the truth, whereupon the Rat branded him a crazy man and had him shot.

The Rat's schemes brought results. In August, 1689, 1500 Iroquois warriors struck the settlement of La Chine near Montreal. The entire island settlement, except for the fortifications, was destroyed. The savages killed 200 persons and took over 100 prisoners, some of whom they tortured before campfires whose glow could be seen by desperate French settlers hiding in the forest across the Chateaugay River.

Count Frontenac, who had just taken charge of French affairs in Canada, decided that the best way to show the Indians and British his strength was to strike at white settlements in Maine, New Hampshire and New York. Three expeditions set out from Montreal in dead of winter, 1690. All returned successful.

The Rat's deceitfulness fell with full force on Schenectady. The real destination of the party of 114 French and 96 Indians which marched down Lake Champlain on the ice was Albany, but the Indians, at the last moment, refused to attack the larger settlement, so the party, guided by four captured Mohawk squaws, made their way to the Mohawk River at Schenectady.

That tiny settlement, barricaded by a strong stockade, was living under false security. Someone neglected to close the gates that night of February 19, probably feeling that the village was in no danger of attack while a snowstorm raged through the valley. It was taken completely by surprise. The settlers awoke to the shrieks of Indians riding high above the howling storm. A few escaped in their night clothes and made their way to Albany, a journey of 15 miles. All but three or four of the estimated 80 houses were burned, 60 people were killed and scalped and nearly 100 taken prisoner. Most of the latter were left behind, only 27 able-bodied young men being taken to Canada. To prove to the Mohawks that the British were their real enemies, the French did not molest 30 braves found in the settlement.

The Mohawks smelled a rat, however, possibly *the* Rat. They lit out after the French, gathering followers as they advanced. The French had almost reached the gates of Montreal when the shrieking Mohawks swooped down on them, killing or capturing 15 men.

THE STARS AND STRIPES

When Fort Stanwix was invested by Colonel Barry St. Leger and his British forces on Sunday, August 3, 1777, the defenders had no official flag to fly from the ramparts, but a Massachusetts detachment which had come to reinforce the fort brought along a newspaper announcing the resolution of Congress proclaiming a national flag for the United States of America. This flag was to consist of thirteen stripes, alternately red and white. In the blue field were to be thirteen stars, representing the new constellation.

The soldiers at Fort Stanwix set to work to prepare a flag. Messengers were sent scurrying about, securing pieces of material from soldiers and from women inside the fort. An ample petticoat supplied the red stripes and ammunition shirts provided the white ones. Since the Third New York regiment, defenders of the fort, wore green and gray uniforms, the problem of blue cloth for the field seemed insurmountable until the men remembered that Captain Abrahm Swartwout had captured a blue camlet cloak at the raid on Peekskill that spring. Swartwout was proud of the coat, but he gave it up reluctantly after exacting a promise from Colonel Peter Gansevoort, the commandant, that he would be repaid later.

Shears and needles flew in clumsy fingers. Stripes of red met stripes of white: strips of blue camlet joined uncertain strips of white in the field. When all was ready the new flag was unfurled from the ramparts and flashed its brilliance of red, white and blue in the bright sunlight of that Sunday morning, a sight which was greeted by the garrison with huzzahs.

The ramparts were crowded when the British appeared in the clearing in full view of the garrison. Orders had been issued to greet the foe in silence. The soldiers were to save their ammunition and to put their time to advantage by counting the numbers of the enemy.

Shrill fifes broke the heaviness of the August air. The drums beat a rat-tat-tat. Line after line of British regulars marched along the edge of the clearing, deploying as they advanced. Their scarlet uniforms, taken out of packs that morning, clung to their shoulders with scarcely a wrinkle. The touches of gold on their hats and sleeves sparkled in the sunlight. And over their heads waved a multitude of regimental banners.

Behind them marched the Hessians, gaily arrayed in green and scarlet, with green cockades in their hats. Sir John Johnson's Greens, irregular both in dress and in precision, brought up the rear.

On the flanks danced Joseph Brant's Indians, hundreds of them, now beating time with the music, now pouring forth war whoops which drowned the fifes and drums. Their painted bodies writhed and twisted, causing a fluttering of the feathers which seemed to grow from their scalps. Ever onward sounded the steps of the regulars, steady, rhythmical, the precision of trained soldiers on parade. And always shining were the shouldered rifles, exchanging flashes of sunlight with the tomahawks of the Indians.

No shout of defiance answered the challenges of the Indians. The regulars and the Hessians passed out of sight along the road to Fort Newport. The shrilling of the fifes sounded to the east, indicating that St. Leger was to camp behind the rise, in the ravine to the northeast of the fort. Johnson and his Greens, accompanied by the yowling Indians, returned to positions near the Mohawk River, where the Indians kept up their shouts for hours.

St. Leger besieged the fort for three weeks. The cocksure colonel had neglected to bring along his heavy cannon, for he thought he could bring the fort to submission by a show of military might and a succession of bombastic notes which Colonel Gansevoort received with scorn.

In the meantime General Nicholas Herkimer and the Tryon County militia marched up the valley to relieve the fort. They were ambushed at Oriskany by Brant's Indians and Johnson's Greens. In one of the bloodiest battles of the Revolution, both sides were forced to retreat, leaving their dead and wounded in a deep ravine.

When St. Leger received news that General Benedict Arnold and a large force of Continentals were marching up the Mohawk Valley to the relief of Fort Stanwix, he pulled up stakes and retreated toward Canada.

He may have taken one last look at the make-shift flag which flew from the ramparts. It may have meant nothing to him, but it represented the spirit of a new nation. It was the first Star Spangled Banner to fly from an American fort under siege by an enemy.

WAR TOUCHES THE FOOTHILLS

The Adirondack foothills held a few scattered settlers during the American Revolution. Indians scalped two children at Mount's Mill near Gray and also raided the isolated settlement of Fairfield. Otherwise, the war touched but lightly on a section to which settlers had not come.

In 1781, when the Mohawk Valley had been riddled by repeated invasions by Sir John Johnson, Joseph Brant, Dockstater and others, the people of Fort Plain sent representatives to Albany to plead with Governor George Clinton that a capable officer be sent to the Valley to organize the militia and repel the invaders. Dominie Gros, a popular preacher, told Clinton that one man and one only was capable of organizing the people and fending off the enemy. That man was Marinus Willett, the hero of the siege of Fort Stanwix and an officer whom the Mohawks and other Indians feared so much that they called him "The Devil."

Willett, though reluctant to give up his rank in the Continental Line, at last consented to renounce any advancement in order to assist the inhabitants of the Mohawk Valley at a time when they were in desperate need of leadership. He took command at Fort Plain, strengthened the fortifications there and at the many other points under his command, and sat down to await a massed invasion of the Valley.

He had just returned from a false alarm at Fort Herkimer when news came that Major Ross and Walter Butler had attacked and scalped several villagers at Currytown, several miles to the south of Fort Plain, and were advancing on Schenectady.

By the night of the 25th of October, his hastily-gathered forces reached Fort Hunter near the mouth of the Schoharie Creek to learn that the invaders were moving toward Johnstown. Willett had 416 men, the enemy 700. The militia climbed the hills from the river and encountered the British, Tories and Indians near the mansion Sir William Johnson had built about ten years earlier and which his son had abandoned at the outbreak of the war.

After sending a detachment of Rowley's Massachusetts men to make a circuit through the woods to flank the enemy, Willett led his militia and a few levies in a frontal attack against the enemy, who began to

9

retreat toward the woods. Suddenly, the American militia became panic-stricken. One man started for the rear, the rest following. Willett rode among them, trying desperately to prevent a rout. He finally succeeded in getting them into order just as Rowley's forces appeared on the field. The enemy, as darkness approached, retreated to the west.

The American force scoured the woods for dead, wounded and trophies of battle. Forty of them had been killed and many were seriously wounded. After rounding up 50 prisoners, Willett led his men to Fort Dayton, now Herkimer, in order to pick up fresh troops for the pursuit of the enemy.

Five hundred picked men and 50 Oneidas waded the cold West Canada Creek a few mornings later and started the long trek through the wilderness. They camped on the old Jerseyfield Road near Norway. A scout detected a light ahead and a reconnoiterer discovered the enemy about to break camp.

The pursuit lasted most of the next day. When the West Canada Creek was reached, most of the enemy had passed over. One officer, however, had stopped for a drink of water. The Indians, recognizing him as the notorious Walter Butler, shot and scalped him. They also stripped him of his military raiment and left his body unburied.

Willett and his men chased the enemy six miles through the wilderness without being able to engage them in battle. Night was coming on. The way ahead was tangled wilderness. With provisions running out and Fort Dayton far behind, Willett called for a retreat.

The people of Fort Dayton received the victorious army with cheers and prepared a banquet on the green for the whole force. On the same day, news came through that Cornwallis had surrendered to Washington at Yorktown, but this victory was completely cast into the shadow by the success of the Willett expedition.

The point on the West Canada Creek where Walter Butler was shot and scalped has long been open to controversy. Some years ago, the State of New York put up a marker indicating that the spot was where the Twin Rocks Bridge crossed the West Canada before the land was flooded to create Hinckley Reservoir. Old-timers living further up the creek say that the logical place was near Flansburg Bridge in Ohio. And, to cap everything, the state got the wrong date on the marker, listing Willett's victory as of 1783 instead of 1781.

HAN YERRY AND THE PAPOOSE

Han Yerry was one of the few Mohawk chiefs who had the courage to remain in the Mohawk Valley after the Revolution. He settled with his wife and family near Oriskany Creek and became quite friendly with Hugh White, the first Pale Face of importance to clear land west of Old Fort Schuyler, now Utica. Together with other Indians, Han Yerry used to come over to watch White and his four sons work on their new home. The Indians found the 250-pound White a congenial fellow, one who was willing to exchange stories of the war and to hand out food to his visitors. A friendship sprang up between the stout Connecticut pioneer and the chief of a dispossessed nation.

One afternoon a group of Oneidas were in the White clearing when Han Yerry arrived. They were young braves who soon tired of watching the house-raising, so they began to wrestle with one another. One tall fellow was always victorious and his confidence knew no bounds, so he walked over to White and challenged him to a bout. White tried to laugh this off, for he was over fifty and outweighed the Oneida by at least 75 pounds. He had been a noted wrestler in his youth and still possessed great strength. The Indian persisted, so White stripped off his shirt and beckoned for the Oneida to come on. This the latter did, boasting loudly as he advanced. As they clinched, White's foot slid behind the legs of his adversary and soon 250 pounds of bone and muscle had fallen upon the Indian. Such weight drove every ounce of breath from the young brave's lungs and it was several minutes before he could climb to his feet and gasp, "Ugh! You good fellow too much."

Han Yerry applauded White along with the other Indians, for the Mohawk chief admired any feat of physical strength. And yet he wanted a real test of White's friendship, some evidence that the Pale Face would trust him.

Several days later Han Yerry arrived at the clearing, followed by his wife and a mulatto woman who helped the chief over the difficulties of communicating his thoughts into English. White's two-year-old granddaughter was playing in the yard. She was her grandfather's pride and joy,

Han Yerry settled himself on the ground and raised a hand. "Broth-

11

er," he said through the interpreter, "you are my friend."

"Yes," White replied, wondering what was coming.

"Brother, if you are my friend, and you believe I am your friend, I shall tell you what I want and then I shall know whether you speak true words."

"Brother, what is it you want of me?"

Han Yerry pointed a finger at the little girl. "Brother, my wife wants to take the little papoose home with us to stay one night, and bring her back tomorrow. If you are my friend, you will now show me."

The request caught White off guard; he had thought that Han Yerry intended to ask for meat or for grain or for some bauble. When the mother let out a cry and clutched the child to her breast, White faced a real problem.

"Brother," he said to Han Yerry, "I believe you are my friend. You may take my granddaughter until tomorrow."

The Whites spent a difficult night. And when morning had been spent and the child had not been returned, the mother wanted the men to go in pursuit of the Indians.

"We must wait," said White. "We would do our friends great injustice if we appeared at their home and demanded the child."

"But they will take her far away. They might even kill her."

"I don't think so."

The sun was slipping behind the trees when a strange procession appeared. At its head strode Han Yerry, his stern face almost broken into a smile. Behind him walked the mulatto woman and Han Yerry's squaw. Atop the latter's shoulders was perched a papoose dressed in doeskin and beads; around its neck hung a huge amulet, and a feather waved from its hair.

Such a disguise failed to deceive the mother of the child. With a cry of joy, she raced across the clearing. The Indian woman handed her the child, who wondered why her mother was shedding tears.

Han Yerry marched straight up to Hugh White and extended a hand which the Pale Face accepted.

"Brother," said the Mohawk chief, neglecting to use his interpreter, "you good man. You my friend. I your friend." Without further ado, he turned on his heel and walked toward the forest, followed by his wife and the mulatto woman.

12

LITTLE PAUL

Drums rolled on the ramparts of Fort Stanwix. Ever higher climbed the American flag, its stars and bars bright in the rising sun. A bugle blared across the Mohawk River. September 22, 1788, had come.

The campfires near the river gave up their glow; they became wisps of smoke over which bent the squat shapes of squaws. An odor of boiling fish mingled with the pungence of the autumn fields.

Powlis, war chief of the Oneidas, sat wrapped in his multi-colored blanket. Today he would sign away his fertile fields along the lazy Mohawk and move toward the setting sun. No longer would he debate the supremacy of Fort Stanwix, which sat like a block of wood in the midst of his lands. In his heart lay resentment against his brother nations.

He refused to give up without a struggle. Throughout a long day of pleading, haggling and threats, he clung desperately to a hope that the Pale Face might spare him. When the sun was preparing to leave the valley in darkness, Powlis gave in. Governor George Clinton wiped the perspiration from his forehead. Powlis envied Clinton the sigh which burst from the depths of his uniform. The heart of the Indian felt no such relief; it lay cold and hard beneath his gaudy blanket.

Drums rolled above the chatter of voices. Powlis and his five sons, sitting dejectedly before their camp fire, raised their eyelids. Governor Clinton was proposing a footrace between the swiftest runners of the Six Nations. A blue and buff soldier climbed the pole on the ramparts and tied to it a heavy bag of gold. Powlis and his five sons grunted and the sound was echoed by the other nations, who quickly chose their best runners.

Powlis waited patiently. The race was being run on what had been his land; it was Indian courtesy that he send his runner to the mark only after the others were ready.

"My sons," he said to the bright-eyed youths, "for the last time we uphold the honor of the Oneidas on our hunting grounds. For this race we must use our speediest runner." His eyes moved around the circle—Flying Eagle, the eldest son, down to Powlis, the fifteen-year-

13

old stripling whom the settlers called Little Paul. He nodded almost imperceptibly.

Surprise and joy lighted the coals which burned in Little Paul's face. He dropped his blanket and stood up. His brown body flashed in the late sun, for his only garment was a breechclout. From the feather on his scalp to the doeskin moccasins which encased his feet, the boy quivered in anticipation of the trial of speed and endurance for which he had been selected. With lithe steps, he made his way to the starting mark, totally unconscious of the sneering remarks about his youth, his thin body and his short stature.

Five towering braves and a stripling toed the mark. The drums rolled as six Iroquois bounded for the distant marker, the half-way point in the race. The Mohawk led from the start, followed by the Onondaga, the Seneca, the Cayuga and the Tuscarora. The spectators jeered at Little Paul, who trailed twenty yards in the rear.

At the quarter mark, the stripling lengthened his stride. The jaunty feather waved proudly in the air which whistled past his expressionless face. The backs of his opponents grew larger as the Mohawk swung around the red, white and blue marker.

Little Paul caught the Tuscarora at the stake and brushed past him with a burst of speed which carried him abreast the Cayuga and the Seneca. The Onondaga, who was tiring rapidly, lurched to the left. Little Paul stumbled and nearly fell.

At the three quarter mark, the Mohawk led by fifteen yards and the Onondaga was breathing hard at Little Paul's shoulder. The Oneida held in no longer. He leaped forward, leaving the gasping Onondaga behind. A hundred yards from the finish he caught up with the tiring Mohawk. Through sheer courage, the older runner matched strides with Little Paul for ten yards before the stripling bounded past him like a young antelope to increase his lead with every stride.

All the pent-up emotion of the day rushed to Little Paul's throat. From his lips leaped a whoop of triumph which was shrill as the cry of an eagle. The unconquerable spirit of the Oneidas rushed with him across the finish line.

As Little Paul stood panting before the Pale Face Governor to receive the bag of gold, the sun of the Oneidas set in a blaze of glory. Old Powlis, watching the scene from his place beside the dead fire, permitted himself one of his rare smiles.

THE INDIAN MOTHER

James Dean, at the age of twelve, had spent several years with a tribe of Oneida Indians at Oquage on the Susquehanna River. While there, he had been adopted by an Indian woman who had lost her son in battle.

Several years after the American Revolution, Dean built a cabin between Cosby's Manor and Fort Stanwix. His home was always open to Indians, whom he considered his friends.

Dean's Indian mother came to tell him that his life was in danger. The Oneidas had been on their annual fishing trip to the Falls of the Cohoes. They had stopped at a blacksmith shop somewhere in the Valley and had taken possession of the fire in order to cook their meal. The owner had ordered them out. A fight had followed, in which the blacksmith had knocked an Oneida over the head with his hammer.

James Dean was familiar with an ancient law which said that if any member of an Oneida tribe was murdered by a representative of another tribe with whom they were at peace, the first person of that tribe to pass through the offended tribe's territory was to be killed. Dean had been the only white man to pass through Oneida territory in a month.

Dean decided to weather the storm. One night he was awakened by the death whoop of the Oneidas. He told his wife to stay in the sleeping room with the children while he went into the main room to await his fate.

Chief Powlis entered the cabin at the head of eighteen chiefs. The light of the candle played upon his face, which was painted black in the Indian manner of symbolizing death. After the chiefs had squatted in a circle, Powlis spoke. The Oneidas had decided in council to take the life of Dean, whom they loved and respected. There was no other way to atone for the murder of their brother at the hands of a white man.

Dean put up a stalwart defense. The law had been made for Indians, not for white men. He had always been a friend of the Oneidas. He had been adopted into their nation. They had given him lands on which to settle. He had built a cabin and had brought his wife and children to live in peace and harmony with the Oneidas.

"Brothers," he cried, "you are wrong. This murder was committed

15

by a Dutchman. He did not speak your language. He did not understand your talk on the Mohawk. He might just as well be called a Seneca or a Tuscarora, merely because his face was red. You can't make me responsible for the doings of all bad white men any more than I could blame you for all the wrongs of all bad Iroquois."

Powlis stirred uneasily. He had long been a close friend of Dean. He asked the white man to retire while he and his chiefs held further council. When Dean was called back, Powlis said, "Brother, we have considered your words. They are like the bark of the beech tree, very smooth, but they do not heal the wounds of our nation. There is a stain on our tribe and it must be washed away with your blood."

"Does our friendship mean nothing?" asked Dean.

"Brother, when I think of our friendship, my heart is soft like that of a child, but no brave will enter the door of Powlis if he does not do his duty, but will point to his house and say, 'That is the home of a woman!' "

Slowly and with great dignity, Powlis got to his feet. His tomahawk flashed as it rose above his head.

Dean did not flinch. His eyes were on a level with the blackened face of the Oneida chief.

The door burst open. An Indian woman rushed into the room and threw herself between Powlis and his intended victim.

"My son," she cried, "I am in time. The tomahawk is not yet red with your blood."

"Go," said Powlis. "You should be home pounding corn."

Dean's Indian mother did not quail when Powlis brandished his tomahawk at her. Two other Indian women had come with her. The three squaws bared their breasts and pressed knives against them.

"Take my son's life if you will," cried the Indian mother, "but you can do it only by passing over our dead bodies. My son's blood shall not run alone."

Powlis' arm dropped to his side. "Brother," he said after a sigh of relief, "we shall go home and have another council." He wrapped his blanket around his tall form and strode out of the cabin, followed by the chiefs and the women.

Dean never learned the result of the council.

16

INDIANS AND INDIAN KILLERS

An elderly resident of Prospect, while wading across the village park one snowy, sub-zero morning, remarked, "It's no wonder the Indians got out and left this climate to us." This unintended tribute probably hit the nail on the head, for there is no record of Indians ever using the Adirondack foothills for a year-round residence. The absence of relics in any quantity seems to support this contention. Indians appeared north of the Mohawk River to hunt and to fish, to tread the warpath and, later, to exchange home-made articles for products manufactured by the colonists.

A Holland Patent historian records that a force of 110 Mohawk Indians led by French officers camped on the Steuben Street hill outside the village on February 1, 1690. Their trail led into the village from the south through the property where the White house used to stand.

Indians also must have used the area for a hunting and fishing ground, for they named the West Canada Creek the Kanata or amber river and described Trenton Falls as the Kuyahoora or leaping water.

Oneida Indians travelled north of Utica each summer for a half century after the Revolution, bartering brooms, baskets, dried venison and fancy articles with the settlers. In South Trenton large parties camped on the Garrett property overlooking the Nine Mile Creek. The bucks would spend their earnings at the taverns, and breaking camp resulted in drunken brawls during which fearful wounds were inflicted with clubs, knives or whatever weapon might be at hand.

The Indians also camped below Remsen, the spot being marked by a large boulder across the Cincinnati Creek from the lower road to Prospect. These Indians evidently made a better impression and one redskin known as Injun Pete saved the property and possibly the lives of a family who had befriended him. He appeared at the door of this home below Remsen one wintry night when the ground was covered with snow. He refused to go to the barn to sleep but insisted on rolling up in his blanket before the fireplace. A shot at midnight drove the family from the loft. Injun Pete stood in the open doorway, a smoking musket in his hands. He told how he had stopped at a tavern in Oldenbarneveld and had overheard two men planning to rob the farmer of money he had saved to build a new house. He had hurried up the hill

17

.

to be there to protect the family. He undoubtedly had driven off some marauders, for morning revealed a trail of blood on the snow.

Indians did not appear too often at Bardwell's Mills, for there lived Green White, a famous Indian killer. One redskin and his squaw evidently had not heard of White, for they drifted in one day and demanded food of a poor farmer's wife. When she refused, the buck took out his tomahawk and began to chop at young trees in the orchard. The woman rushed after White, who came on the run. He levelled his flint-lock musket at the Indian's heart and pulled the trigger, but the woman struck up his arm and the ball entered the side of the cabin above the Indian's head. White, disgusted at this lack of gratitude, contented himself by scolding the woman and telling the Indians to "git goin'."

White also enjoyed a reputation as a hunter with a quick temper. While hunting with John Bonner, a huge man, he started an argument and insisted on finishing it with a fight. Bonner laughed, for White scarcely reached to his shoulders. White insisted and for a short time used his nimbleness to pelt Bonner merrily, but the larger man finally got a grip on his adversary, slammed him to the ground and sat on him. White, after struggling vainly to extricate himself, growled, "Bonner, what's the use to fight? There's no one to see who whips." Bonner got the point, released the clever White, and the two pioneers walked home together, firm friends.

The most famous Indian killer once lived at Old Forge. Nat Foster has become almost a legend and he may have been the prototype for James Fenimore Cooper's Natty Bumpo. He fought Indians all his life and ended up by killing an Indian named Peter Waters but familiarly known as Drid. Foster's two day trial for murder, held in Herkimer in September, 1834, attracted much attention, for it was the first test of the right of an Indian in a white man's court. There seems no doubt of Foster's guilt, but the evidence was too circumstantial to convict him. When the jury came in with a verdict of not guilty, Foster rose to his feet, turned dramatically to the court room, stretched both hands over the heads of the spectators and cried, "God bless you all! God bless the people!"

Part II

PIONEERS

THE LAST DAYS OF A BARON

Baron Friedrich Wilhelm von Steuben, the most important Revolutionary War figure to settle in the Adirondack foothills, came in the summer of 1787 to land holdings deeded to him by the State of New York. He and his friend, William North, cut their names on a big tree while they watched the surveyor, James Cockburn, divide the land into lots. On his way back to New York, Steuben wrote from Fort Plain: "Here I am this far on my return. I have spent sixteen days at Steuben. I have gone all over my lands and am enchanted with them. The soil, the exposure, the climate, all meet my wishes."

Steuben probably did not visit his holdings again for several years, for he was in financial distress, but he made arrangements with Samuel Sizer, a ship's carpenter from Springfield, Massachusetts, to clear some land, put up a cabin and also erect a sawmill.

Congress granted Steuben a pension of $2,500 a year in 1790, so he set out for his land holdings. The trip from New York took twelve days, three of them being consumed in making the trek through the wilderness from Fort Herkimer to Steuben. He probably came up the Mohawk to the Nine Mile Creek to a point where he expected a road to be cut by Sizer from that creek to Steuben.

Sizer evidently had not been too efficient. Steuben's diary reveals the general's disappointment: "The mill is no further along than last year, the dam is broken and there is little likelihood that the mill can run in three months, consequently the West House is not finished for lack of timber. Not one acre has been cleared as it should be for the sixty acres. The boat I confided to Sizer's care has been lost through his neglect. The road to Nine Mile Creek for which I paid Sizer four dollars a mile, aside from bridges, is in bad shape for lack of repairs, which would not require more than three or four days of work. Finally he has not set foot on my square and far from attracting settlers to Steuben it seems as though his indifference has even discouraged those who are already established here."

Possibly the Yankee carpenter was able to divert the Baron's wrath by presenting a bill for unpaid services, for Steuben, shortly after his arrival, settled upon Sizer $20 in cash, a barrel of pork, a barrel of flour and 100 acres of land.

The Baron envisioned a manor in the wilderness, for he had set aside 800 acres for his own use. Though the stocky ex-officer with the short legs was over sixty, he evidently felt that many years lay ahead for him. He enjoyed coming each summer, to watch the laborers clear the land, to witness the erection of cabins. He first tried leasing land, but the settlers would have no part in that scheme, so he began to sell it, usually at a dollar an acre. Payments were irregular and the Baron found himself short of cash most of the time.

His home consisted of a log house containing three rooms. His constant companion was a young man named Mulligan who acted as his secretary. Friends visited occasionally, particularly William North and Benjamin Walker, who had been the general's aide during the war. Of the twenty-odd settlers who came to his lands, several were veterans of the Revolution, and Simeon Woodruff had circumnavigated the globe with Captain Cook. The Baron's closest friend was Captain Simeon Fuller, a man in whom he placed complete confidence. One day when Fuller reported the loss of his lease, the Baron turned to Mulligan and said, "Make out another lease. Mr. Fuller is hard at work. I hear the trees falling on his lot each day."

The Baron lingered at Steuben longer than usual in 1794. In late November he came down with cold and fever. Mulligan called the neighbors and a messenger was sent for a doctor, probably to the Mohawk Valley. The doctor arrived the day after Simeon Fuller had closed the Baron's eyes in death.

The Baron left a will, bequeathing certain amounts to his neighbors and co-workers. In it was a rider which shocked his neighbors: "That on my death, they do not permit any person to touch my body, not even to change the shirt in which I shall die but that they wrap me up in my old military cloak and in twenty-four hours after my death, bury me in such a spot as I shall before my death point out to them, and that they never acquaint any person with the place where I shall be buried."

He was buried, supposedly under a hemlock tree. Ten years later the body was moved to its present location in the grove behind the replica of his log house erected within recent years by the State Education Department.

GENERAL FLOYD AND THE MEASLY PIG

General William Floyd, who came to Westernville in 1803, was the only signer of the Declaration of Independence to settle in the Adirondack foothills. He purchased 40,000 acres in the present towns of Floyd and Western, built the colonial mansion which still stands on the main street of Westernville, and spent the last 17 years of his life there.

Floyd had never been a famous military man. His rank of general had been gained in the militia before the Revolution. His contribution to the war was primarily legislative, for he served in the First Continental Congress which met in Philadelphia in 1774 and sat on numerous committees. He owned a reputation for patriotic ardor and for faithfulness to the cause of liberty. His opinions were formed after long periods of thought and reflection and he was not easily swayed from his way of thinking.

In Westernville he occupied the position of wealthy landlord to a group of poor pioneers. His generosity knew no bounds, with the result that his frugal wife often checked up on him. One day a farmer asked for grain, so the general went to the granary, measured out a bushel of wheat, and gave it to him. Floyd's wife put up a strenuous objection, saying that the general was forever making gifts without investigating the needs of the recipients. He listened to her tirade before turning to an assistant and saying, "Go measure out another bushel of wheat and give it to that poor man. This gift is from my wife, who wishes to share in the giving."

The general was able to sift wheat from chaff. One settler leased a plot of land but, due to downright laziness, did not make enough money to meet the payment at the end of the year. This fellow, knowing the general's sympathetic nature, brought along his only cow and a hard luck story.

"How many children have you?" asked Floyd.

"Five, but they are too young to help me."

"Aye! Aye! Five small children, and you too lazy to support them. Drive the cow home and go to work. Earn some money to pay your rent."

Slavery was legal in New York when General Floyd moved to

Westernville, so he brought a number of Negro slaves with him. Two anecdotes about these slaves have come down through the years.

Bill, the general's favorite, rode over to Fort Stanwix one Independence Day to celebrate. The speeches he heard there were filled with talk about the equality of man. Bill pondered deeply about this equality as he tippled at every tavern on the way home, and came to the conclusion that, if he were equal to Floyd, the general should get out of bed, unharness his horse and turn it out to pasture.

He rode up to the gate and hallooed.

The general opened a window and asked what he wanted.

"I want Massa Floyd to turn out this horse," Bill yelled.

The general chuckled as he caught the thickness in Bill's speech, so he called back that he would be right down. He dressed, came down, and with great ceremony unharnessed the horse and turned it out to pasture, while Bill went to bed to sleep off his new-found independence.

A second Negro, known as Long Tom the Hunter, was particularly adept at ridding the premises of foxes. At slaughtering time, the general was dismayed to discover that his prize pig, which weighed 400 pounds, was diseased with measles and could not be sold, so he offered the carcass to Long Tom to be used as fox-bait.

Tom led the pig away, supposedly to the slaughter, but he had other ideas. After dark he hitched up a team of horses, hoisted the "measly pig" into the wagon, and drove to the store of one Brayton, a Yankee merchant who had a reputation of being shrewd as a fox. Brayton examined the well-fattened pig and paid Tom the top price for it. The Negro rode home, jubilant at having out-witted the store-keeper.

General Floyd was scarcely out of his bed the next morning when Brayton pounded at his door to accuse him of palming off a "measly pig" on him.

"What!" exclaimed Floyd. "That Negro hasn't sold you that measly pig? I'll call the rascal."

Tom answered the summons but insisted that the general had given him the pig.

"How did I tell you to use it?" Floyd asked.

Tom's lips spread in a wide grin. "Massa Floyd done give me the measly pig to bait foxes," he said, "and I caught the biggest fox in town with it."

MR. BOON WAS IMPRACTICAL

Gerrit Boon, the first agent of the Holland Land Company, was probably the first white man to fight his way over the Big Hill (Deerfield Hill) from Old Fort Schuyler (Utica) to Oldenbarneveld. It is said that he blazed the trail by marking trees with an axe. He found sap running from the maple trees when he arrived at the junction of the Steuben and Cincinnati Creeks, so he came to the conclusion that it flowed the year round.

The Holland Land Company, which he represented, consisted of a group of Amsterdam business men who were thrilled with the idea of building up an industry which could compete with the cane-sugar business in the West Indies, so they gave their agent a free hand.

Boon, who envisioned a sugar bush of 10,000 acres which would produce a million and a half pounds of sugar each year, hired two dozen Yankees to cut out all but the maple trees on the slope overlooking the two creeks. Conflict arose immediately, for the wood-choppers held lumbering ideas of their own. Boon, impatient and stubborn, discharged half the crew and brought in new choppers. The air rang with the sound of axes that summer of 1793, with the result that seventeen acres were made ready for the next run of sap.

The Yankees had always carried the sap to the vats in buckets. Boon scorned this primitive method. He built a mill on the Cincinnati Creek, incidentally to furnish lumber for houses, but primarily to provide wood for troughs to carry the sap down the slope to the huge vats being made to await it. The mill proving useless for the latter purpose, Boon spent the following winter in Albany, where he found a woodworker who was willing to construct troughs according to his specifications.

The troughs were installed on the hillside the following February. Boon tapped the trees and a complicated system of troughs was devised to carry the sap to the vats at the foot of the slope. Here he ran into more trouble, for the specially-manufactured troughs were thin-walled and could not withstand the alternate freezing and thawing. They began to warp and much of the sap was lost through overflowing and leakage. Boon abandoned them in favor of crude grooved slats manufactured at his own mill. These slats did not warp, but the sap did not run down them freely and the strips could not be nailed tightly enough together to prevent sap from leaking.

He produced but 3,000 pounds of maple sugar that year, so he rode off to Philadelphia to talk the matter over with Casenove, the general agent of the Holland Land Company. Cazenove, who favored the sugar experiment, was unwilling to abandon the enterprise, but the stockholders, who had suffered a loss of $15,000, thought too much money had been expended for such meagre results, so the books were closed on November 30.

Undaunted, Boon went ahead to build up an ideal settlement at Oldenbarneveld. He set about establishing sawmills, gristmills and stores. The three-story gristmill below the settlement on the Cincinnati Creek was 50 by 60 feet in size and could accommodate five runs of stone. Unfortunately, the creek in summer was not powerful enough to turn the wheels. If Boon had not been so insistent upon building in Oldenbarneveld, he could have constructed a mill on the West Canada Creek a few miles away, but he clung to his way of thinking. The mill, which had cost the company $9,000, was inventoried in 1815 at $1,500.

Boon was not around to see this depreciation. His mills and stores had lost money, and he had been unable to get payments from farmers for whom he had cleared land and erected homes. It being his policy to bring the best class of settlers to Oldenbarneveld, he had made advances in the form of subsidies as follows: tinsmith $300, lime-burner $1,300, hatter $150, quarrier $100, shoemaker $100, blacksmith $600, mason $300 and physician $100. He had also advanced to his friend, Francis Adrian Van der Kemp, that most learned and delightful of scholars, the sum of $800, merely because Van der Kemp was a Dutchman and a scholar, and also assumed debts contracted by his equally impractical friend.

These frills brought the wrath of the stockholders down on Boon's shoulders. When Cazenove was succeeded by Busti as general agent in 1798, Boon was recalled to Holland. He turned over his affairs to Adam Mappa, his assistant, and sailed away never to return, but his name remains on the land, for Boonville, a frontier settlement he founded, perpetuates his memory.

DUTCH SCHOLAR

Governor DeWitt Clinton of New York, on April 20, 1822, penned a letter to an elderly Dutch gentleman in Oldenbarneveld: "I shall go to the West early in June to visit the whole line of the canal, and, if possible, I will make a diverging visit on my return to the most learned man in America."

Clinton arrived in Oldenbarneveld to encounter two old gentlemen fishing for trout in the Cincinnati Creek. One of them was Colonel Adam Mappa, land agent for the Holland Land Company; the other, Francis Adrian Van Der Kemp, was the man to whom he had addressed the letter.

Mappa and Van Der Kemp, friends of long standing, were exiles from The Netherlands, where they had participated in an unsuccessful revolt against the government in 1786. They were intellectual and moral giants who stood opposed to tyranny in any form. Together, they succeeded in making Oldenbarneveld a settlement where men could exercise freedom of conscience, both politically and religiously.

Van Der Kemp and Clinton also had much in common, for the Dutch refugee was probably one of the first men to see the importance of an inland waterway through New York. In 1792, two years after his arrival in America, he had explored the territory from Fort Stanwix to Oswego and later had settled for some time on an island in Oneida Lake. His long and interesting letters written to Mappa at the time give a wonderful estimate of the resources of the state and show how beneficial a canal would be in developing them.

The Erie Canal, when completed under Clinton's direction, did not follow Van Der Kemp's route, but Clinton, after reading one of the Dutchman's letters, wrote: "It gives you the original invention of the Erie route, and I shall lay it by as a subject of momentous reference on some future occasion."

Van Der Kemp, the scholar, was employed by Clinton in translating the early Dutch records of the Colony of New Amsterdam into English. The man from Oldenbarneveld also kept up a correspondence with celebrities, among them John Adams and Thomas Jefferson. Adams had been instrumental in bringing Van Der Kemp to America. His letter of introduction had brought the Dutchman an invitation to visit Mount Vernon, where Van Der Kemp found Washington cold but courteous and Mount Vernon a place "where simplicity and order, unadorned grandeur and dignity, had taken up an abode." And Jefferson, but six months before his death, wrote Van Der Kemp, telling of his increasing age and failing eye-sight and hoping that his friend might "continue to enjoy good health and a life of satisfaction."

Anecdotes about Van Der Kemp are legion. He was evidently near-sighted, absent-minded and impractical. While living in Esopus on the Hudson River, he decided to cut down a tree. Clinton, seeing him working awkwardly at the task, donned workmen's clothes, took up a scythe and made a pretense of mowing. After working his way close to the tree, he put down his scythe and remarked, "Ah, Meinherr Van Der Kemp, you can no more cut down that tree than if you were a woodpecker." Van Der Kemp prepared to argue with the workman but, when his eyes got into focus, he recognized Clinton beneath the disguise and saw that his old friend was playing a joke on him, so they both threw down their tools and enjoyed a good laugh.

One day in winter, when Van Der Kemp had business in a village near Oldenbarneveld, he climbed into his sleigh and clicked to his horse. After driving for some miles, he suddenly came upon a settlement. There was something strangely familiar about the houses, so he stopped a man and asked the name of the village.

"Oldenbarneveld," replied the man.

Van Der Kemp shook his head with unbelief. "Ah, but that may not be," he said, "as I have just left there."

While living at Oneida Lake, he wanted to build a new chicken-house. To do so, he had the frame hewed on the banks of the Hudson and rafted all the way to Oneida Lake, though he was surrounded by virgin forest. Again, after reading about the latest methods in agriculture, he planted some beans. Much to his surprise and chagrin, the plants came up with the beans on top, so they had to be turned over in order to make them grow according to Nature.

The two friends, Mappa and Van Der Kemp, were separated in April, 1828, when the Colonel passed away. Van Der Kemp lived until September 7 of the following year. Both are buried in the Oldenbarneveld Cemetery on the Mapledale road.

BOON'S BRIDGE

Early settlers used the fording place above Prospect Falls in travelling to and fro from Russia to Prospect. At best, the crossing was hazardous and, in time of flood, impassable. When the State Road was built from Albany through Johnstown, Salisbury, Norway and Russia to the West Canada Creek between 1805 and 1807, the fording place was no longer adequate to handle the traffic, so a bridge was thrown across the chasm below Prospect Falls. This structure, which had no central pier, was an engineering feat which astounded the pioneer settlers. It was supported by limestone blocks piled tightly against the walls of the chasm.

This first bridge, which was named Boon's Bridge after the first agent of the Holland Land Company in Oldenbarneveld, saw service during the War of 1812, when troops passed over it en route to Sackets Harbor. These soldiers were poorly-equipped and ill-fed. They camped one night near the stone house in Russia now owned by Donald Mc-Grath. The night was cold and many of the men tried to hide in the house and barn to keep warm until they were discovered and driven out by officers. They also created a nuisance for Andrew Cady, who lived on what is now the Clemons farm on the road from Prospect to Remsen. Cady, being patriotic, had saved milk from the dairy and his wife had baked huge quantities of bread, beans and other food. After the troops had passed, nothing was left of these provisions, and the Cady orchard had been stripped of its fruit.

According to Prospect tradition, a cannon was dropped off the bridge by the passing army and lies at the bottom of the deep pool below. About fifty years ago an old man named Sam Hemstreet used to come to Prospect each summer from the Rome County Home to interest listeners in schemes of his own for redeeming this relic.

The first bridge evidently proved to be a headache to the town of Trenton. On March 4, 1817, it was resolved to petition the legislature to make the bridge a county charge, and in the next year another petition was sent to Albany "Praying assistance in rebuilding Boon's Bridge." And on January 25, 1820, the following lengthy resolution was passed by the town: "Whereas it appears to be the sence of this meeting that the bridge commonly called Boon's Bridge across the West

29

Canada Creek and connecting the State Road leading from Johnstown to Sackets Harbour is so much out of repair that it is rendered dangerous to pass and therefore become highly necessary that a new one be erected as soon as possible, the peculiar situation of the place & no other more convenient will create such an expense, that this meeting deem it proper to petition the Legislature of this State now in Session for pecuniary aid in such a sum as they in their wisdom may think proper to grant." Whether a second bridge was constructed at this time, it is impossible to determine, but in 1828 the town voted that all bridges should be covered with good and sufficient covering, recommending hemlock shingles as the best. It seems highly probable that Boon's Bridge became a covered bridge at that time.

Boon's Bridge lasted until 1869, when a year of exceptionally high water undermined the foundations and made the building of a stronger bridge necessary. It was torn down and replaced by an iron bridge which in turn gave way to the present concrete structure in 1930.

Boon's Bridge will linger in memory as long as legends endure. While the bridge was under construction a farmer from Russia, thinking it passable, rode across on horseback on the stringers in the darkness, not realizing the extent of his feat until Prospect villagers brought him back to view the slim boards thrown across the chasm. The story does not tell whether the farmer returned via the same route or chose the safer fording place above the falls. The story has been elaborated to make the traveller a small girl who tottered across, hovering over the chasm in midpassage, much to the horror of bystanders.

The iron bridge also has its legends. Three farmers came over from Russia to celebrate the conclusion of a successful haying season. Late at night, when the trio had finished at Arnold's Hotel, they started home. An argument took place as to the location of the bridge. Two of the men were right. The third miscalculated, landed in a rubbish heap and had to be rescued before he slid into the rushing creek.

On another occasion the justice of the peace was waiting to serve a legal paper on an old lady who was accused of harboring some transgressors of the law, including some boys of her own. The old lady was also vigilant. She spied the justice and hurried for the bridge in order to cross to Herkimer County, where he had no authority. He gave chase, but it is said that the old lady outlegged him.

DAUGHTER OF AN EMPEROR

The story of Caroline Charlotte Benton reverses the old rags to riches tale. She was the illegitimate daughter of Joseph Bonaparte, former King of Naples and of Spain, and Annette Savage, daughter of pious Quakers in Philadelphia. Her childhood was spent in extreme luxury. She died penniless.

Joseph Bonaparte left his wife behind when he came to America after his brother Napoleon had been exiled to Elba. He shipped as M. Bouchard and wished to remain incognito, but he had been in New York but a fortnight when he was stopped on lower Broadway by a Frenchman who dropped to his knees, kissed Bonaparte's hand and called him Your Majesty. Bonaparte no longer chose to conceal his identity and took up residence in what is now Clermont Inn on Riverside Drive.

We next find him in Philadelphia, living at Lansdowne House, where he took the name of Count de Survilliers, the name by which he was known during the 15 years he spent in America. Life in Philadelphia might have been tolerable for this ex-king if he had not wandered into a Quaker shop to buy a pair of suspenders and seen Annette Savage, the daughter of the proprietor. For Annette it was a case of love at first sight; she overthrew all her Quaker scruples by going to live with Bonaparte as his mistress. Popular disapproval by Philadelphians drove them from the city and they took up residence at Point Breeze near Bordentown, New Jersey.

Here Joseph, who was tired of courts and intrigue, lived like a country gentleman. When offered the throne of Mexico, he turned it down. Evidently his wife and family did not look askance at his intimacy with Annette, for his daughter, Princess Charlotte, spent three years with them at Bordentown.

Bonaparte made his first trip into the North Country in 1818 to visit Le Ray de Chaumont and to take a look at land he had acquired some years before while in France. The story of this acquisition bears repeating. It seems that Joseph, who had been ousted as King of Spain, returned to Paris with $125,000 worth of jewels and art treasures. Le Ray went to see him, hoping to get him to invest in American land. Joseph, afraid that his stolen gain would be confiscated, traded the

31

jewels and art treasures to Le Ray for 26,840 acres of land in America.

Joseph liked what he saw in Northern New York and soon returned to build four mansions in the wilderness. It was at his main house in Natural Bridge that Caroline Charlotte was born. Life was happier for the mother at Natural Bridge, for here the people called her Mme. Bonaparte. The little girl lived in luxury, surrounded by the best of French furniture, catered to by servants, partaking of the best food.

She had reached the age of 12 when the bubble burst. Another revolution had taken place in France. Joseph Bonaparte left his half-built summer place at Alpina and went back to France.

Annette and her daughter took his departure philosophically. The mother married Joseph de la Foille, a former valet in the household. Though Bonaparte had left her a considerable sum of money, her new husband went through it recklessly. They left Evans Mills and opened up a shop in Watertown. When de la Foille died, Annette married Harry Horr and finished up her days in New York.

The little girl who had grown up in luxurious surroundings caught the eye of Zebulon Benton, the poor son of a physician from Oxbow. She married him and lived to regret her decision. Benton put on great airs as son-in-law of an ex-king and squandered the money Bonaparte had settled upon his wife. Charlotte, as she was usually known, left him and took up school-teaching in Watertown.

When Napoleon III ascended the throne of France, she took her daughter, Josephine, to Paris and gained an audience with the King to present her credentials. Napoleon III took one good look at her and said that her face was proof that she was a Bonaparte. He declared her birth legitimate and made Josephine a maid-of-honor to his wife, Empress Eugenie.

Charlotte and Josephine enjoyed ten happy years in France. With the establishment of the French Republic after the Franco-Prussian War, Charlotte found her pension cut off. She returned to America and lived in comparative obscurity.

When she died in poverty at Richfield Springs in 1890, her passing hardly brought mention. She is buried at Oxbow on what had once been her father's land.

LADY IN WAITING

A row of trees near the Black River at Deferiet marks the site of the Hermitage, a gray stone mansion with pillared veranda which once housed a great lady who wore around her neck a locket containing a miniature of Mme. de Stael and who claimed to have been a lady-in-waiting to the Queen of France.

Jenika de Feriet had emigrated to New Orleans with her mother and two brothers at the outbreak of the French Revolution. Here Baron Ferdinand, the elder brother, became a prominent business man and remained in this country after the rest of the family returned to France at the close of the Revolution. The other brother, Gabriel, closed a checkered career which embraced saloon-keeping, gambling and soldier of fortune when a boat he was using on a smuggling expedition collapsed.

Jenika probably returned to America through the influence of James Le Ray de Chaumont, who was opening up large tracts of land in Northern New York to settlers. She arrived in 1816 and spent several years as a guest of the Chaumonts at Leraysville.

Construction of the Hermitage began in 1821 and Jenika took herself off to New Orleans to visit her brother. She stayed seven months, but the climate did not suit her, so she returned to supervise the furnishing of her home, which was ready for occupancy in the spring of 1824.

The Hermitage, approached from the rear along a driveway cut through the forest, contained furnishings sent from France. Jenika, who was a skilled musician, owned the first grand piano in northern New York, also a Grecian lyre, a harp and a violin. Her love for plants was reflected in a large conservatory, where blossomed orange and lemon trees and exotic plants from various parts of the world.

Though Jenika never married, she assumed the title of Madame, a recognized custom for middle-aged, unmarried ladies who owned their homes, and it was as Mme. de Feriet that she entertained royally at the Hermitage. Her fame as a hostess spread through the North Country and her home became a stopping place for musicians, writers and conversationalists.

Mme. de Feriet, an excellent horsewoman, rode far and wide through the countryside, visiting friends and going over her estate.

Her occasional trips to Watertown always caused a flurry of excitement, for she was a good spender at the stores. She also attended all social events and her gowns, designed and made in France, created quite a sensation.

Like many of the emigres, she seemed to have no sense of financial responsibility. She had thrown all of her funds into her land purchases and the building of the Hermitage, expecting settlers to rally round her banner. Unfortunately, she had chosen the wrong side of the Black River from the highway. People were not anxious to settle on land that had to be reached by fording a stream. She had a wooden bridge built across the river and later replaced it with one which had stone piers.

She had been in the Hermitage but two years when the financial pinch began to creep up on her. She could not pay her installments to the Chaumonts and their continual pressure brought a complete break in their hitherto friendly relations. Deprived of their friendship, she found herself outside the social whirl. And when the Chaumonts and others left for France in 1832, she felt alone in the wilderness. Her nephew, Gabriel, came to attend Lowville Academy and spent his vacations with her, thus offering a temporary respite from the homesickness which was beginning to overwhelm her.

The Hermitage was put up for sale in 1836, chiefly at the insistence of her brother Ferdinand. No cash offer was forthcoming and she did not care to exchange her home for more land. She travelled to New Orleans to consult Ferdinand and spent a year there. The climate again distressed her so she returned to the Hermitage, spent a year in straightening out her finances, and set sail for France in 1841.

She did not find happiness there. Most of her old friends had died. The court did not contain its former splendor. Probably it ignored her, for she was now poor and in bad health. Her earlier genius for pleasing people evidently had left her along with her wealth. She died at Versailles less than two years after her return to France.

The Hermitage stood until 1871, when it was levelled to the ground by fire, but the French lady's name still remains in the attractive village which bears her name.

AND FROZE TO DEATH

The most notorious year in our history, climatically speaking, was 1816, the famous "Eighteen-Hundred-and-Froze-to-Death." The whole world seemed to feel the effects of the unseasonable weather. Even the heart of Africa shivered. No month failed to produce a frost. Lake Erie was not clear of ice until May. A blizzard hit Vermont on June 17, completely blocking the roads with drifted snow. Maine got six inches on the 22nd of July. A frost late in August killed off most of the corn in New York and New England.

The Adirondack foothills are noted for their cold climate. An old-timer in Prospect once described weather in that village as "nine months of winter and three months of damned poor weather."

Storrs Barrows, who served as village historian of South Trenton for many years during the nineteenth century, wrote down his recollections of 1816, a year which he endured while a youngster.

"January was very mild. The mean temperature was higher than any January since.

"February was not very cold, excepting a few of the last days.

"March—Cold, boisterous, piercing winds, with drifting snow; after the 20th milder; furious freshets; river swollen; Mohawk flats covered with water. Boats were used from near Deerfield Corners to the village of Utica.

"April came in quite warm and balmy, but as the month advanced the cold increased, ultimately ending with a winter's temperature instead of spring.

"May—Oh! how chilly. Buds and fruit were frozen. The 18th day Co. Hicks planted his corn the second time with an overcoat and mittens on. Corn was planted and replanted until anticipations of a crop were no more.

"June—Our latitude is N. 33 deg. 10 min. This was the coldest June ever known in this latitude. The 28th day Charles Gouge and John Younglove (the last named gentleman a resident of Utica) were chopping a hemlock tree some three feet in diameter; at the heart of the tree they found ice. There was a sprinkling of snow here on the 25th.

"July—Snow fell to the depth of six inches in Maine on the 22nd of July. There was frost and ice on the 4th. I wore my overcoat to attend

'Independence', Francis A. Bloodgood, orator. Indian corn was nearly all destroyed. There was not one sound ear in Oneida County. We had to depend on seed corn raised in 1815 for the spring of 1817. It was worth six dollars a bushel.

"August, if possible, was more disagreeable and cheerless than the summer months already gone. The 16th ice was formed as thick as window glass· Almost every green vegetable was destroyed. In England they called 1816 the year minus a summer.

"September—From the 5th to the 19th was the mildest weather of the season. After that to the 30th was very cold. The mercury ran down to 28 degrees. For a number of nights it fell below the freezing point.

"October was famous for cold nights—Frost, ice and snow made our fingers tingle in gathering the potato crop. Snow on the 13th fell to the depth of eight inches. It lodged upon the trees. Rain fell and the snow was frozen, forming heavy loads; consequently the branches were unable to sustain the great weight, and forest and fruit trees were badly broken.

"November was in keeping with her sister months. Old rude Boreas, the blustering railer, was constantly with us. Snow fell on the 10th so as to make good sleighing; the 12th the stage passed on runners.

"December was more favorable, very much so. The average or mean was above many subsequent Decembers. A very comfortable month for out door business.

"Thus I have given a brief abstract of the year 1816. That was a cold year. Frost in every month· Old 'Sol' refused to give his accustomed warmth during the summer months. The price of grain was very high and scarce—wheat flour $16 per barrel. Many a person went to bed supperless. I know whereof I affirm."

Part III

THE STATE OF RELIGION

WELSH PIONEERS

In early summer, 1795, a tiny caravan left Fort Schuyler, now Utica, crossed the Mohawk River and made its way toward the land which had been granted to Baron von Steuben by the State of New York. It consisted of a lead horse, four oxen drawing a loaded cart or wagon, and eighteen members of five families who had left Carnarvonshire in North Wales early that March.

There was no road leading into the Adirondack foothills. Two years earlier Gerrit Boon had traced a route from Fort Schuyler to Oldenbarneveld by marking trees with an axe. The Welsh found a settlement at Oldenbarneveld and a crude road had been constructed along the banks of the Cincinnati Creek to what is now Remsen.

The five Welsh families reached the Steuben grant four days after they had left Fort Schuyler. The Baron had died the preceding November. Samuel Sizer, his assistant, was in charge. He and the Yankee settlers near Sixty Acres were friendly toward the immigrants, though most of their transactions must have been carried on in sign language, for the Welsh had but a few words of English and the Yankees knew no Welsh.

Of the pioneer Welsh, Owen Griffiths is the only one about whom much is known. He became the father of the first Welsh child to be born in Oneida County. He also conducted the first store which, because of its color, was known as *store felen* or the yellow store·

These Welsh pioneers were not political leaders, fleeing from the wrath of a king, or religious zealots, searching for a place where they could worship God in their own way. They comprised uneducated men and women who sought in America a chance to better their lot economically. Conditions in the British Isles were deplorable. A succession of wars had drained the treasury. Heavy taxes were bleeding the people. Poverty and starvation became common among the poorer classes. Schooling was practically non-existent and child labor was on the increase. It was to avoid such a path that the Welsh had turned their backs on their beloved Wales and had chosen a road which, difficult though it might be, held promise for the future.

Most of the Welsh settled in the hills, which may have reminded them of their native country. The land was not fertile. Much of it was forest. Mosquitoes and black flies were so thick that brush was burned continually to smudge them out. Stones lay everywhere. The economical Welsh cleared them from the fields and used them to make boundaries for their holdings. Grain was planted and harvested, but the Welsh soon realized that the soil was not adapted to these crops.

They turned to dairying, for grazing lands were plentiful and corn, hay and oats seemed to thrive in the stony soil. Buttermaking became the chief industry. Most of the butter was churned in the homes. Farmers marketed their product in two ways. The local merchants were buyers and shippers of butter. Owners of large farms dealt with butter-merchants who took the entire product of the dairy to New York in the autumn. Inasmuch as these men seldom returned before spring, farmers ran up bills at the stores and hoped for the best. There was one fellow who came back with tears in his eyes and sobbed that butter was piled on the New York wharves to such a height that one couldn't see the tops of the buildings. He hadn't been able to get a cent for the butter, but he reached into his pocket and produced a snuff-box as a gift to the housewife to show his good faith. Welsh butter, often called Oneida County butter, established a reputation in New York which endured for nearly a century. Cheese also was made, but not on a large scale.

Quarriers soon discovered that the banks of the Cincinnati and West Canada Creeks contained a plentiful supply of limestone, which was in demand for building purposes. Houses constructed of native stone became common around Remsen, but most of the stone was used for foundations, gate-posts, steps and hitching-posts. Stone-cutters were kept busy carving opened books, wreaths, little lambs and Welsh inscriptions on gravestones which lent a touch of immortality to those who had passed on.

Shop-keeping did not appeal to the early Welsh settlers, for they did not approve of Yankee shrewdness. A story is told of a young Welshman who entered into partnership with a Yankee in Prospect. He endured Yankee ingenuity for several years, but when his partner insisted upon putting different price labels on two spouts which led through the wall into the same molasses barrel, the Welshman pulled out and opened a store in Remsen, where folks evidently were more honest.

CHAPELS ON THE HILLS

The Welsh who settled in the Adirondack foothills early in the last century arrived in the wake of one of the greatest religious revivals ever to sweep Wales. George Whitefield and John Wesley had broken with the Church of England. They, together with Christmas Evans, John Elias and other preachers, had travelled through the rain-swept valleys, swaying the people with fiery oratory. Self-governing Calvinistic groups sprang up all over Wales, and this spirit of religious independence crossed the Atlantic with the early settlers.

The Welsh had been in Steuben but a short time when they built a log church and school. This building, named Ebenezer, was levelled to ashes on a Christmas morning three months after it had been opened. Since the courage of a Welshman rises in proportion to the obstacles thrown in his path, it is not surprising that the settlers had a frame church built the following summer and replaced it in 1818 with the stone church, *Capel Ucha*, which stood on the hill overlooking Remsen for over 80 years and was then replaced by the abandoned church which now stands there.

Chapels sprang up all over the Steuben hills during the next half century: *Capel Isaf*, or the Lower Chapel, *Capel Coch*, which had a brief but hectic existence, *Nant* or *Cobin*, French Road, Bethel, *Pen Y Graeg*, *Enlli* and *Capel Bont*. Remsen raised Whitefield, or the Stone Church and later, after an altercation between him and his parishioners, Rev. Morris Roberts collected funds to build *Peniel*, now the Remsen grange. Holland Patent had two Welsh churches, Trenton one and South Trenton one. Prospect had three, the Moriah Congregational, the Welsh Calvinistic and the Welsh Baptist.

The most important chapel historically stood on the road from Prospect to Fairchild. This chapel, *Pen Y Caerau*, established in 1826, became the first Welsh Calvinistic Methodist church in America.

The chapel was the cornerstone of Welsh life. Quarrels between members were referred to the chapel for adjudication. A tribunal of elders or deacons usually decided a case, but sometimes the whole membership body sat as a court. Pastors as well as church members could be disciplined. One preacher stirred up such a hornet's nest by picking a mess of peas on the Sabbath that he was forced to resign his pastorate.

41

And a young girl who innocently decorated her bonnet with flowers received a scolding which she probably remembered for the rest of her life.

The Welsh, like the Puritans, observed Sunday religiously. The Sabbath began at sundown on Saturday. No food was cooked on Sunday and only necessary chores were performed. Much of the day was spent at chapel. Afternoons in the homes were devoted to Bible reading, discussions of the morning sermon and individual prayer. After evening chapel the family reassumed the secular tasks of the week.

Welsh preachers made up in enthusiasm what they lacked in scholarship. Their sermons were long and emotional, the high point being the *hwyl,* when the preacher, literally "under full sail," tugged at the heartstrings of his congregation with an outburst of musical oratory which evoked cries of *Gogoniant,* Hallelujah and Amen.

The Welsh might have been devout, but they were not impressed with mere oratory. A revivalist once came to *Enlli* to convert a few stubborn souls who had resisted all efforts to bring them into the fold. His flowery speech swayed all but one dour Welshman who remained in his seat when the preacher invited the congregation to come forward and repent. In response to a special invitation, the lone character asked, "Is it right this minute I must be saved?" He was not saved, at least on that day.

The Welsh considered singing next to Godliness. The chapels had no organs. The hymnals contained no notation. A leader lined the hymn; that is, he announced the meter, sounded the pitch with a tuning fork, and chanted the first line; then the congregation sang, not in unison, but in four parts. This minor harmony, as it floated across the hills and valleys, was filled with haunting beauty. .

The highlight of each year was the *Gymanfa,* or preaching festival, which was usually held in September. On these occasions the Welsh pushed aside doctrinal differences which kept them apart and joined together in two days of religious revival. In 1843 Rev. Henry Rees, then the outstanding preacher of Wales, drew such a crowd to *Capel Ucha* that a platform had to be built outside the chapel windows and Mr. Rees preached both to the people inside the stone building and to the crowd which filled the chapel yard and flowed over onto the sloping hillside.

THE BELOVED PREACHER

Most preachers in Welsh chapels were uneducated men who made up for their lack of scholarship with a display of emotional zeal. In strange contrast was Rev. Robert Everett, who settled in Steuben in 1838 as pastor of *Capel Ucha* or the Upper Chapel. He had received his training at Wrexham Seminary in Wales and had preached successfully in Utica, West Winfield and Westernville, he having left the last-named village after a fire had destroyed his home and his valuable library. His home a mile from Remsen on the road to Steuben also burned, but years after his death. A state marker indicates the site.

Dr. Everett—he received an honorary degree of Doctor of Divinity from Hamilton College in 1861—was forty-seven years old when he came to *Capel Ucha*, but he threw himself into his task with tremendous energy. He not only preached at *Capel Ucha*, but he established another Welsh Congregational church on Pen Mount. Every Sunday afternoon, rain, shine or snow, he preached in the tiny wooden building, long since torn down, called *Pen Y Mynydd*.

An earnest reformer, Dr. Everett espoused the cause of total abstinence and was prominent in forming temperance societies in Remsen and Steuben. His interest in humanity led him to involvement in the abolition movement and his home became a station on the Underground Railroad. Opponents exposed him to ridicule and personal insult. On one occasion pranksters cut off the tail and mane of his horse.

In 1853 Dr. Everett and his son translated Harriet Beecher Stowe's best-seller, *Uncle Tom's Cabin,* into Welsh. Paper-bound copies circulated through the Steuben hills, and much of the enthusiasm of the peace-loving Welsh toward the Civil War may be attributed to this translation, a rare copy of which may be seen at the Didymus Thomas Library in Remsen.

Dr. Everett's unblemished character and his pure scholarship won him the admiration of people wherever he preached. His understanding of the frailties of human beings and his sympathetic nature made him the most beloved preacher ever to fill a pulpit north of Utica.

He was an avid reader and a prolific writer. In order better to take notes from his readings, he invented one of the first systems of shorthand, which he used in both English and Welsh, and published a

43

book of instruction in the latter language. Together with two others, he compiled a hymnal which was used by Welsh chapels for many years. He also prepared a Welsh reader for Sabbath schools. His outstanding literary contribution, however, was a Welsh magazine, *Y Cenadwr Americanedd* or *The American Messenger,* which had a wide circulation in Wales and the United States for over 40 years. This magazine was printed in the preacher's home, with his son assisting.

Mrs. Everett, a wholly unselfish woman, had a gift of business ability which her husband lacked and was able to manage the house and a family of eleven children on the preacher's limited income. The children all received fine educations; two of the girls became well-known teachers while one son, trained as a preacher, set up a flourishing daguerreotype business in Utica.

Dr. Everett was 84 years of age when he preached his final sermon at *Capel Ucha* two weeks before his death. His courageous wife tried to carry on his magazine with the assistance of a son, but she was thrown from a sleigh three winters later and suffered injuries which contributed to her death in 1878.

The *Utica Morning Herald,* in recording Dr. Everett's passing, said in part: "As a clergyman, the denomination to which he belonged has, by common consent, given him the first place in its councils; his advice has always been respectfully heard, and generally followed. This has been very marked among the ministerial brethren; men almost as old as himself have looked up to him as a father, and their regard for him has been largely veneration for one who seemed to breathe a purer spiritual atmosphere than is given to other men. He semed to fill his place naturally, and as a matter of course, without effort and without strife. He was not eloquent, but rather diffident in the pulpit; though the inspiration of his theme, with which he was always in sympathy, made him a pleasing speaker, and sometimes kindled an enthusiasm more eloquent than the most eloquent oratory. His judgment was keen and his convictions strong; but in presenting the most abstruse subject he was so largely sympathetic that he was always very near to those he addressed."

44

THE MADOGIANS

The Welsh in the Adirondack foothills got quite stirred up during the first half of the nineteenth century by reports from the West that tribes of White Indians who spoke pure Welsh were wandering around in a state of godlessness. These Indians were called Madogians, and were supposedly direct descendants of Madog ap Owen Gwynedd, a Welsh prince who had discovered America in 1170. He had returned to Wales and gathered a fleet of ten ships and 300 followers. They had sailed into the west, never to return, but the Welsh felt that they had landed again in America and that these white Indians were their survivors.

Welsh scholars had been attempting to establish Madog as the true discoverer of America for centuries. During the reign of Elizabeth I of England (1558-1603) a Welsh scholar named David Powell boldly proclaimed that the country Madog had discovered was Mexico, and the shrewd monarch used his published work as evidence to support her claim to Spanish lands in America. Both Hakluyt and Raleigh, her favorite world travellers, chose to mention Madog's discovery in books they had published.

James Howell, a true Welshman, while languishing in Fleet Prison, improved on the Madog story by incorporating into one of his articles the following poem, which supposedly was inscribed on the Welsh prince's tomb somewhere in the West Indies:

> "Madog lies here, descended from the blood
> Of Owen Gwynedd. Long upon the sea,
> I rather chose to brave the ocean's flood,
> Than to own lands in their immensity."

Rev. Morgan Jones, while travelling in the Tuscarora country of South Carolina during the seventeenth century, was taken prisoner and condemned to death. Jones, shocked by such a fate, said in purest Welsh, "Have I escaped so many dangers to be now knocked on the head like a dog?" Much to Jones' surprise and relief, the Tuscarora chief embraced him and told him in Welsh that he would be saved. Again some cantankerous scholar spoiled a good Welsh story. Said he, "If Mr. Jones, a man who left South Wales in the seventeenth century, could talk intelligibly with the descendants of people who had left North Wales in the twelfth century, he or they must have been endowed with the gift of tongues spoken of in the Holy Writ."

Despite this slap, the Welsh kept trying. Welsh-speaking Indians were encountered on the Red River and beyond the Mississippi, and one Joseph Roberts reported that he had heard a white Indian swear in pure Welsh. Another Welshman reported that there were 50,000 Welsh Indians near the source of the Missouri River.

James Owen of Trenton wrote to a friend in Wales in 1819: "I think, if we live a little longer, the door will be opened for us to find out about the old Cymry. We are determined to make every effort to find them out. We are almost sure that they may be found in the Mud River, twelve miles from the Missouri. Next week we are to collect money to send a man to them. We have many ready to go, but we have decided to send John T. Roberts, who was born near Denbigh, Wales." Of the Welsh Indians, Mr. Owen wrote: "The men are said to have reddish hair, and the women to be very comely."

Roberts went with a companion as far as St. Louis, where he talked with people who had travelled the length of the Missouri River. He reported to the folks at home that the Indians out there did not understand a word of Welsh but they did not like the sound of the language, for they invariably stuck their fingers in their ears when Welsh was spoken.

Remsen wasn't cured by this revelation. A man named Percy came through about 1837 and told how he had discovered white Indians in Patagonia near the tip of South America. He left with a considerable sum of money but never returned to Remsen.

As late as 1856, a correspondent to the Welsh magazine, *Y Cenadwr,* pleaded with his countrymen to search for Welsh Indians who might be talking "in our dear, old language and holding Eisteddfods somewhere in the northwest."

He didn't get much response. Critics were calling the Madogians Mad Dogs, and folks were sick and tired of sending money out on lost causes. A few still clung to their banner, but, as one writer phrased it, "Those Welshmen who still cling to the old belief do so, as it were, with the fingertips of their intellects."

46

THE STATE OF RELIGION

Rev. John Taylor, a missionary from Hampshire County, Massachusetts, travelled north of Utica in 1802 to determine the state of religion among the pioneers, many of whom had emigrated from New England.

The first settlement he visited was Floyd, where he found 130 families and 800 inhabitants. There was no meeting house, but Presbyterian, Baptist and Methodist societies flourished. He found the Methodists fascinating and wrote in his Journal: "There has been, and is supposed, an awakening among the methodists. They have their quarterly meetings, sacraments, and love-feasts. The last meeting was on the 4th of July—had their sacrament in the woods—began their meeting on Saturday morning, and continued until Sunday night. There were 6 preachers present. In this meeting 6 persons fell down—in a manner similar with the falling down in Kentucky—and after lying 20 to 30 minutes, rose, crying glory to God. Some of ym appeared to be senseless—others in great agitation. These persons appear to the present time to be very pious."

Mr. Taylor talked with two of the persons who had been struck down and found that their descriptions of their feelings were "something unaccountable." He preached to an audience of 100 people comprising all three sects, found the people attentive and kind and departed with their good wishes—but with no contributions.

At Trenton he stayed with Rev. Mr. Fish, a circuit-rider who earned a meagre reward for preaching in the village and outlying settlements. Mr. Taylor, discouraged because the school children had no catechisms or necessary school books, sent an order for "24 Bibles, 10 catechisms, 4 of Janeway's Tokens, and 10 of Dodridge's Addresses" and gave Mr. Fish permission to distribute them.

The missionary found Steuben religious. A church, formed the year before, had 30 members who were regular attendants at services. He liked this settlement so well that he stayed nearly a week, preaching to the people, attending schools and visiting with families. He discovered that the people, though poor, were very considerate and, though the schools were destitute of books, the children were making progress toward good order and good schooling.

47

Remsen did not get such a clean bill of health. Either the people were bad or Mr. Taylor felt a bit cantankerous, for he wrote of this village: "This is a broken society. The people are very ignorant and very wicked—about 3 months since a stranger came into the town, who appeared to be a pert coxcomb, about 28 years of age, who calls his name Alexander. He soon obtained a school, and in about a fortnight set up preaching, and he pretends to preach every Sabbath. Who and what he is they know not—but that he is some notorious villain I believe there is no doubt. Many of the people—especially the wickedest part—are very much attached to him. There is no chh. in town, and but one professor, who belongs to the chh. in Steuben." Some of Mr. Taylor's rancor may be attributed to the fact that his own lecture attracted not more than 25 persons and, by his own admission, "a number of those were far from being decent in their behaviour, and it was not in my power to make them feel reproof nor the force of truth."

At Western, Mr. Taylor stayed for some time with General William Floyd, then about 70 years of age, but retaining the full powers of his mind. The missionary found the land fertile and the crops excellent, but he deplored the fact that most of the land was leased and not owned. "If men do not possess the right of soil," he wrote, "they never will nor can feel independent." He also thought the people were in a poor situation as to religion and order. "They are, a few excepted, extremely ignorant," he confided to his diary, "and the ignorant methodist preachers are leading them into errors and all kinds of disorder."

General Floyd did not take such a pessimistic view of the situation. He told Mr. Taylor that the Methodists were making great strides and appeared to be doing as much good as harm. Before their arrival the people were living in a heathenish state, and the activity of the Methodists was forcing other sects to rouse themselves. Sixty people attended Mr. Taylor's lecture at a nearby hamlet, causing him to write: "I think that if I have at any time made good impressions it was on this evening."

RUSSIAN LANDMARK

Visitors driving through the West Canada Valley almost invariably point to a pillar of white which shines like a beacon when the afternoon sun strikes it. Natives inform them that they are looking at Russian Union Church, probably the most important landmark on the hills overlooking the creek. Though 136 years old, it still serves the community.

It was on June 9, 1820, that William Walters, Russia carpenter in charge of building the church, climbed to the twelve foot spire which then surmounted the present octagon-shaped steeple, opened up a bottle of brandy, touched it to his lips, swung it around his head three times, and broke it over the spire of the completed church. Such an act might seem sacrilegious today, but customs of that time dictated that all buildings be so dedicated.

The Russia Union Church was really a community venture, for six Protestant sects participated in its erection and shared the use of its auditorium. The Open Communion Baptists and Presbyterian groups, being the largest in number and support, each used the church two Sundays a month, while the Methodists, being but two, had the privilege of holding service there only on the fifth Sunday of April. Other denominations which used the church were Episcopalians, Closed Communion Baptists and Universalists.

Pews were contracted for a month before the dedication of the church. No man contributed more than $200 and some of the poorer settlers gave as little as $7.50. One 21-year-old, Abner Moon, contributed his entire summer's earnings, ninety dollars, toward the building of the church.

Among the pew holders were Amherst Coon, the first white male child to be born in the village, eight known veterans of the American Revolution and several men who had served in the War of 1812, incluing two officers. The following business men also owned pews: William Graves, after whom Gravesville was named; Stoddard Squire, who ran a sawmill on the West Canada Creek; Abel and Philo Rust, the first men to quarry lime in Russia; Asa McMaster, proprietor of a tavern in Prospect; Adam Frink, Russia storekeeper; and Stephen

Smith, who ran a tavern at the top of Buck Hill and served as justice of the peace for the town of Russia for over forty years.

The original church, in addition to the spire, which was blown away by a hurricane in 1850, had an auditorium 45 feet square and an entrance lobby from which stairs led to a gallery which ran around three sides of the church. The front seats in this gallery were reserved for choir singers, and the singing in the Russia Church was famous for years. There is no record of the first service, but the sermon was probably delivered by Elder Benajah Crop, an 83-year-old preacher who had organized the Baptist Society in 1799 and continued to serve until 1826.

Despite the fact that several religious groups had cooperated in building the church, there evidently was no love lost between the sects. For example, some of the offenses for which Baptists were ordered to appear before a conference "to have their walks in life examined" were "Attending Universalists meetings and patronizing their papers" and "uniting with the Methodist Church."

The Russia Union Church had its ups and downs. The Baptists were unable to afford pastors at certain times. The Presbyterians, who also owned a chapel, depended upon supply preachers during most of their existence, which ended with the Civil War. The Universalists, a small group, erected a brick building in Gravesville which is now owned by the grange. The Methodists, who found their numbers greatly increased by Civil War revivals, joined the Black River Conference. Together with the Baptists, who supply the preacher, they make up most of the present congregation.

The church underwent physical changes. As the congregations declined, the gallery was closed and a large room was provided above the auditorium for town offices and for social events connected with the church. The long horsesheds, which had served their purpose, were torn down.

On Sunday, August 24, 1930, the church celebrated its 110th anniversary. Among the 500 people in attendance was a daughter of one of the original pew-holders. The gathering proved so successful that "Old Home Day" has become an institution in Russia.

WOMAN WITH COURAGE

One of the first two white women to cross the Rocky Mountains was brought up on the Fox Road a mile and a half from Holland Patent. Little is known of Eliza Hart's early life except that she joined the Presbyterian Church in Holland Patent in 1828. She married Henry Harmon Spalding and went with him to the Lane Theological Seminary in Ohio, where he was preparing to become a missionary.

In 1836 another missionary, Marcus Whitman, who planned to cross the Rockies to convert the Indians of Oregon, asked the Spaldings to go with him. Spalding did not make up his mind immediately, for he had once proposed to Clarissa, now Whitman's wife, and had been turned down. It was Eliza who made the decision. After praying alone in her room, she decided that "they should change their destiny to the Rocky Mountains."

Eliza was a woman with courage. She knew that there would be friction between her husband and Clarissa, a beautiful, blonde woman who had been educated at Mrs. Emma Willard's Female Seminary in Troy and who had a voice "sweet and musical as a chime of bells." Eliza was practically an invalid, for she had recently recovered from a stillbirth and subsequent illness. Yet she was filled with religious spirit and felt that it was her duty to aid Henry in rescuing the unenlightened.

They set out with a fur caravan, a group of men whose crudeness must have been painful to the two women. Most of the journey was made on foot, on horseback, or in a two-wheeled cart. Eliza slept on the ground and subsisted on a diet largely of buffalo meat which finally made her deathly sick. She was so exhausted and ill at one point in the journey that she pleaded with the others to go on and leave her to die, saying, "Do not put me on that horse again." She felt sure that her mother in Holland Patent would understand.

Clarissa Whitman enjoyed excellent health. She ate ravenously of meals which John McLaughlin, the Hudson Bay Company's factor, served them, roast duck, fresh salmon, sturgeon, boiled pork or tripe, with apple pie and pudding for dessert. She chose to ignore the sulk-

51

ing Henry; and Eliza, sure that he was loyal to her and to her alone, forced herself to continue the journey.

The Whitmans and Spaldings parted company at Vancouver. Marcus and Clarissa settled among the treacherous Cayuses, while Henry and Eliza travelled 120 miles to join the peaceful Nez Perches. Here Eliza established classes in weaving and knitting and Henry, in addition to erecting sawmills, became the founder of the modern delicacy, the Idaho potato.

The Nez Perches liked the Spaldings. After their first baby was born, the Indians would snatch the little girl from Eliza's arms, and often the mother would have to pick fleas off the child when the Indians had finished fondling it. The child was a Godsend to Eliza, who had not seen a white woman for a year until Clarissa came to help her with the birth of the child. Clarissa had borne a child eight months earlier, so the two women forgot Henry's moodiness in their common love for their children.

The woman from Holland Patent who, in contrast with Clarissa, was tall and plain with a coarse voice and little education, appealed to Whitman's wife, who wrote of her: "I have always loved her and felt as if no one could speak against her."

Clarissa's child was drowned. She also became ill and her eyesight began to fail. The Cayuses were unruly, for their ranks had been swept by a measles epidemic and Whitman, who was something of a doctor, had stemmed it too slowly, with the result that the Indians thought he had poison in his medicine kit.

That year little Eliza Spalding was ten, so she was sent to Whitman's mission for her schooling. She had scarcely arrived when the Indians struck. Whitman and his wife were murdered and the little girl was held prisoner. Henry, in an attempt to rescue his daughter, was driven off. It was a month before the child was returned "too weak to stand, a mere skeleton and her mind as much impaired as her health." Henry, saddened by the affair, wrote a long, realistic letter to Clarissa's parents and enclosed a lock of their daughter's hair.

Eliza Hart Spalding, whose frail health had been ruined by years of toil among the Indians, sickened and died. She was buried in a land three thousand miles away from the Holland Patent of her childhood. She stands as a symbol of the sacrifices made by pioneer missionaries.

CAMP MEETING

Methodists of the Utica and Herkimer districts held camp meetings during the Civil War in a grove near the West Canada Creek south of Poland. The Rome District group gathered in a grove a quarter of a mile north of Prospect station on the Black River & Utica Railroad. Neither of these places proved satisfactory, so in 1867 the Rome District Camp Meeting Association purchased from James Reeve and John C. Frank a plot of 33 acres on the road leading from Trenton to Poland. This property included an excellent grove on the Cincinnati Creek.

The first Camp Meeting held there, on September 9, 1869, attracted the largest religious gathering ever to be held in Oneida County. Some people came the night before and pitched their tents in the grove. Others began to arrive at seven the next morning. The *Utica Morning Herald* estimated that from 20,000 to 30,000 people attended the preaching services at ten, one, three and seven o'clock.

This meeting, and those for thirty years afterward, took place in the Old Circle. The "Preachers' Stand" accommodated 40 ministers and the congregation sat on rude benches made of spruce boards. It is said that these seats were so uncomfortable that few listeners could fall asleep without falling off, and it was even hazardous to swat a pestiferous mosquito without losing one's balance.

A colony of 150 tents sprang up each summer on the Camp Ground. There were no floors to these tents, so most of the campers slept on damp bedticks. Five tons of straw were used annually to fill these ticks. Old photographs show groups gathered in front of these tents, most of which had names such as "Home" or "The Beeches" or "The Maples."

Improvements came gradually. Eliphalet Remington of Ilion arms fame built the first cottage, and the tabernacle which replaced the "Preachers' Stand" was erected in 1899. A combination boarding hall and store went up in 1875 and another large building served as a storehouse for lamps, stoves and tentpoles.

It also served as a jail for transgressors, for the Camp Ground was run on a strict basis, and small offenses might be punished by imprisonment. Law and order was in the hands of the trustees, who patrolled the grounds, wearing large badges on their coats. Their hands were often full, for pranksters from nearby villagers thought it considerable sport to upset preaching sessions, and a constant vigilance had to be maintained to drive off these intruders.

Admission to the Camp Ground was fifteen cents for one horse and wagon and twenty-five cents for a team, regardless of the number of people in the wagon. A tollgate stood at the entrance to the grounds for the collection of these fees. Later, season tickets were sold at thirty-five cents a head. The Camp Ground was closed on Sundays for a period of ten years, for the Association did not feel justified in charging admission on the Sabbath.

While Camp Meeting was in session, rows of rigs lined the fences on either side of the road to the grounds. Runaways were common, and it was evidently quite a sight to see a red-faced driver trying to quiet frantic beasts as they pranced between the rows of rigs with slight regard for the sanctity of the occasion.

Life throughout America underwent a radical change with the coming of the automobile. People were no longer satisfied with spending time in peace and quiet. The Camp Ground became a victim to the age of speed. Admissions no longer paid for improvements, so taxes were levied upon tents, cottages and barns. Electricity replaced lamps in 1913 at a cost of $1,000 and better sanitation came in 1932.

A severe blow hit the Camp Ground on April 28, 1922, when fire of undetermined origin swept through it. Twenty-four cottages and the combination boarding hall and store were totally destroyed.

The Association, badly in debt, was ready to quit. Here the campers took a hand. A Cottage Owners' Association sprang up to help in the maintenance of the grounds. Fences were repaired, roads kept in condition and trees planted. Later improvements included a tennis court and a swimming pool.

A gate, erected about 1939, makes an attractive entrance to what is now known as Trenton Assembly Park, or "T. A. Park," according to the inscription on the mailbox. Campers still come each summer, some to spend the entire season in the attractive cottages.

PART IV

GROWING PAINS

THE LEAPING WATER

One summer day in 1805 a solitary hiker left the Oldenbarneveld clearing, forded the Cincinnati Creek at Parker Hollow and took the trail which led across the high land to the West Canada Creek. He made his way with difficulty, for the path was poorly defined and recent storms had thrown trees across it. The underbrush grew so thick in places that he had to crawl on hands and knees to get through it.

He probably stopped frequently, not only to catch his breath, but to ease his tormented mind, for the life he had planned so carefully had been broken at the age of 33. He came from a prominent Connecticut family. His grandfather had been a signer of the Declaration of Independence. His father had served as a captain in the American Revolution. The hiker himself had graduated with honors from Yale College and had gone to Mansfield eight years before to become the pastor of the First Church in that Connecticut village. His first years there were eminently successful. His kindly manner and liberal ideas appealed to the younger people, who accepted his teachings wholeheartedly. The older folks tolerated him for a while but, when he began to preach Unitarianism as opposed to the Trinitarian doctrine, murmurs of discontent arose. The Association of Ministers of Windham County got wind of what was transpiring in Mansfield, asked the young preacher to recant and, when he refused, expelled him, not only from their organization, but from all "Ministerial Connexion."

The young minister came to Oldenbarneveld to visit his cousin. He preached before a newly formed Unitarian society in that settlement and was invited to locate there as permanent pastor. He faced two choices: he could return to Mansfield, where a majority of his parishioners favored him despite the ruling of the higher-ups, and preach before a congregation that was split by dissension; or he could come to Oldenbarneveld at a small salary and help to further the cause of Unitarianism in a frontier settlement.

One can only imagine his thoughts as he struggled through the wilderness, emerged at Carmichael's Point and saw for the first time the cataract which the Indians called Kuyahoora, the Leaping Water. Here stood the bewildered minister who had been driven out of Connecticut by well-meaning people who were not sufficiently enlightened to grasp what his quick mind was thinking. Before him lay the amber river, unchained and unharnessed, plunging one hundred feet over limestone cliffs before rushing toward the sea between cedar-covered walls, the very symbol of the things for which he stood.

The hiker must have done some deep thinking as he plodded back to Oldenbarneveld, and the trip to the falls may have influenced his decision for, early in the next year, he accepted the call to Oldenbarneveld and moved his wife and two small children there. He preached in Oldenbarneveld and Holland Patent for four years, but the income was too small to support his growing family, so he resigned his charge and set up a school in his home outside the village. His teaching was as liberal as his preaching, and he found time to write and publish a grammar in which he denounced former methods of teaching and introduced progressive ideas of his own. During these years he was saving and planning, in order to have for his own the glorious cataract he had seen on his first visit to Oldenbarneveld.

His dream came true in 1822, when he purchased 60 acres along the west bank of the West Canada Creek and built a home which he called the Rural Resort. He improved the means of seeing the falls by blasting out rock and installing staircases and protective chains to aid tourists in climbing through the chasm.

Two eminent visitors arrived in 1824. Philip Hone, the famous diarist, had been Mayor of New York. Dominick Lynch's name has been given to the main street of Rome. These men suggested that the minister enlarge his house to accommodate overnight guests. When he pleaded poverty Hone loaned him $5,000 and the improvements were made.

The minister published a pamphlet describing his falls and encouraging travellers to visit the Rural Resort. The response exceeded his fondest expectations. The house was filled most of the summer and the family was kept busy conducting parties through the gorge.

The courageous minister was not destined to reap the reward, for he died four years later at the age of 56. He lies in the grove on the hilltop behind where his hotel once stood, a few rods from the powerhouse at Trenton Falls.

The inscription on his tombstone reads: "Sacred to the memory of Rev. John Sherman, A.M., who departed this life Aug. 2, 1828, aged 56 years.

THE OLD SOW

Motorists driving through Turin seldom notice the antiquated cannon which peers timidly at them from a pedestal on the village green. A close inspection would reveal the inscription on it: "1812-1912." Some research would establish the fact that the cannon was the first to be fired in the Second War against Great Britain.

When that war broke out, Sackets Harbor became a naval and army base for military operations against Canada. Part of the limited equipment was a cannon which the British had brought to America in 1689 to help in their struggle with France for control of this continent. It had turned up at Fort Ticonderoga during the American Revolution and Ethan Allen, after capturing that outpost, had ordered the cannon hauled off to Boston, where General Henry Knox used it in the defense of Dorchester Heights.

At Sackets Harbor it was set up in a tiny fort on the plateau overlooking the harbor. Sackets Harbor boasted few regular troops, most of the defenders being militiamen under the Quaker general, Jacob Jennings Brown. When the British sailed into the harbor in July, 1812, the militia hurried in to defend the little fort. These impromptu soldiers dubbed the cannon "The Old Sow."

The Old Sow was a 32-pounder and the only balls available at Sackets Harbor were 24-pounders, but this obstacle did not disturb the ingenious Yankee defenders. They scurried around the village, collected old pieces of carpet, and wrapped the balls in them. When the British demand for surrender was refused, the enemy flagship took a shot at the fort, but the ball dropped into the harbor.

The Old Sow responded with a loud roar, but the carpeted missile did not carry to the flagship, much to the chagrin of the defenders. The British continued the bombardment unsuccessfully, while a battery of smaller guns from the shore pounded away at smaller British ships. The stalemate went on for two hours.

The British aim had been for the most part short, but suddenly one ball whizzed over the heads of the defenders and fell beyond them with a thud. It was a 32-pounder! The militiamen scampered to retrieve it and rammed it into the Old Sow's maw while a sergeant cried, "We've ketched 'em out now, boys. Let's send it back!"

The Old Sow proved equal to the occasion. Its ball struck a mast of the royal flagship and sent it flying into the harbor. The British commander, crippled by his own ammunition, gave the signal to withdraw. The Old Sow, with one shot, had scattered a fleet and saved Sackets Harbor.

It took the Harbor about 100 years to appreciate what the Old Sow had done. The citizens recalled that Zebulon Pike, the explorer, was buried there, that Ulysses S. Grant had served his apprenticeship at Madison Barracks near the site of the Old Sow's miraculous feat. Assistant Secretary of the Navy Franklin D. Roosevelt came to the Harbor to dedicate a commemorative monument. But where was the Old Sow?

They discovered the cannon perched on its pedestal on the green in Turin, and assumed that it had been stolen, so they asked the Navy Department to have the cannon restored to the Harbor.

The Turin folks refused the request. The villagers owned the cannon and could prove it; they liked the Old Sow and were not going to relinquish it.

It seems that the United States government sold a batch of outmoded military stores as junk to G. Lord of Watertown in 1851 and the Old Sow went along for the price of 1400 or 1500 pounds of old iron. After wandering over to Croghan, it finally came into the hands of W. L. Babcock of Lowville.

Turin, being a patriotic village, wanted some kind of cannon with which to celebrate Independence Day and other occasions which demanded a loud outpouring of sound. A subscription was taken up and a leading citizen, Emory Sackett, went to Lowville and purchased the Old Sow. Whether the Turin patriots knew the historical value of the piece is debatable, but the villagers heard the Old Sow's bellows every Fourth of July for many years and during the Civil War celebrated every Union victory with a bang.

Turin is not giving up the Old Sow. If Sackets Harbor cherished the old cannon, why did they sell it for junk? And, furthermore, if the Turin folks wanted to sell it, who would have the right to do it?

GENERAL TRAINING DAY

Between the War of 1812 and the Civil War, civilian protection was carried on by the state militia, which consisted of all able-bodied men between the ages of 18 and 45, though exemptions could be claimed by state officers, clergymen, teachers, firemen, sailors and students at colleges or academies.

The militia rested on a democratic basis. Only generals and staff officers were appointed by the governor. The militiamen elected their own captains and subalterns (lieutenants) by ballot, and these officers in turn chose the colonels of the regiments. It was the duty of each commanding officer to enroll all men in his jurisdiction and to notify them of the time and place for general training.

This general training took place once a year, on the first Monday of September, and might continue for several days. Officers also met in June or July for special instructions, as did the company musicians.

The villages in the Adirondack foothills all held general training. In Prospect the troops were trained on the village green by Major J. A. Reeves, the village cabinet-maker and undertaker. Holland Patent devoted four days to drill and merriment on White meadow under Colonels Aaron White and A. S. Bagg and Captains Charles Willard, Simeon R. Fuller and William Ralph. The Remsen militia gathered at the upper tavern and marched through the streets to where the present railroad depot stands. Here they were drilled by Colonels Matthew Beecher and Griffith Jones.

The center of activity was Trenton, where Colonel John Billings, a veteran of the War of 1812 and for many years the village postmaster, put the recruits through their sprouts. The whole countryside turned out. The taverns served roast pig, baked beans and brown bread, while the youngsters made themselves sick on gingerbread and spruce beer, a concoction made from spruce, dandelion and wintergreen.

A veteran of general training in Herkimer left an excellent account of such a day in his village. "Although the companies exhibited the *elite* of our regimental splendors, glittering with tinsel and flaunting with feathers, a more heterogeneous and unsoldierly parade could scarcely be imagined. There were the elect from the mountains, who sometimes marched to the rendezvous barefoot, carrying their boots and soldier clothing in a bundle—the ambitious cobblers, tailors and plough-boys from cross-roads hamlets and remote rural districts, short, tall, fat, skinny, bow-legged, sheep-shanked, cock-eyed, hump-shouldered and sway-backed—equipped by art as economically awkward and variously as they were endowed by nature, uniformed in all contempt of uni-formity, armed with old flint-lock muskets, horsemen's carbines, long squirrel rifles, double-barrelled shot-guns, bell-muzzled blunderbusses, with side-arms of as many different patterns, from the old dragon sabre that had belonged to Harry Lee's Legion, to the slim basket-hilted rapier which had probably graced the thigh of some of our French allies in the Revolution. This harlequinade of equipment, costume and char-acter was duly paraded twice a day, marched through the streets, and put through its maneuvres on the green commons adjoining the village, much to the satisfaction of all emancipated school-boys, ragamuffins, idlers, tavern-keepers, and cake and beer venders, and somewhat, per-haps, to the weariness of industrious mechanics who had apprentices to manage, and busy housewives who depended on small boys to help."

A. M. Maxwell, a British tourist en route to Trenton Falls, ran into general training day in Utica in 1840. "In Chancellor Square," he wrote, "we saw more military maneuverings; and certainly more awkward gentry I never beheld; but what can you expect, when only three days in each year are set apart for instruction? The chaps, not-withstanding the blustering of their military mentor, were all whiffing cigars and amusing themselves. I admit that some of the uniform companies are in a much better state of discipline. Their dragoons remind me of the times of Oliver Cromwell; for these cavaliers have red jackets, or jerkins, cut in the oldest fashion, with yellow doublets, and yellow breeches, and immensely long red feathers, stuck on most uncouth-looking caps. We had 'Patrick's Day' and 'Yankee Doodle' from every band we fell in with; and where there was no band, an outrageous thumping of drums supplied the deficiency."

The commanding officer regulated the sale of liquor on the grounds, and most of the officers were inclined to blink an eye on total absti-nence. General training day usually ended up with wet celebrations, and roads were filled with jubilant militiamen well into the following morning.

THE IRON HORSE

At quarter to ten on the cold, blowy morning of December 13, 1855, two trains crowded with invited guests left Utica for the first run of the Black River & Utica Railroad to Boonville. The first train, which consisted of six yellow coaches carrying a band, a military corps and the most important guests, was drawn by a pot-bellied, wood-burning locomotive named the *John Butterfield*. Behind it puffed a second train of cars drawn by the *Daniel C. Jenne*.

Snow cluttered the track and the heavy trains made slow progress. Stops were made at Stittville, Holland Patent, Trenton, Remsen and Alder Creek. Villagers turned out en masse to greet the iron horse and to admire the yellow coaches and the top-hatted dignitaries, while they listened to marches played by the Utica Brass Band. Something special was added at Holland Patent, where a corps of militia fired a salute from a cannon.

Boonville, then the terminal of the line, put on a real show. Houses were decorated with red, white and blue bunting. Across the main street stretched a huge banner which contained the slogan of the railroad: "The Black River & Utica Railroad. It can and must be built!" Sleighs of all description whirled back and forth through the streets, all converging near the present village park, across from which the station was located.

Around noon every church bell in the village began to toll. Boys ran here and there, shouting and cheering and yelling, "It's coming! The iron horse is coming!" And, sure enough, far down the track near the Black River Canal crossing, a cloud of smoke appeared above the wide funnel of the *John Butterfield*. The whistle shrieked a warning, causing ladies to cover their ears. Horses pranced and snorted in terror as the train rolled in, shaking the crude platform with its vibrations. Showers of sparks belched from the funnel, causing the crowd to scatter. The *John Butterfield* wheezed to a halt, while its bell tolled in unison with the deeper sounds from the church spires.

The band and a corps of militia in gaudy uniforms climbed from the first cars. While the musicians blared forth marches, the *Daniel C. Jenne* arrived with its larger load amid the rousing cheers of the spectators. Richard Hulbert, the hotel proprietor, came from the station, dressed in a swallow-tailed coat and a tall hat. After shaking hands with a group of important-looking gentlemen, he mounted a soapbox and made a long, flowery speech, the first of several that were delivered. When the ceremonies were at an end, all of Boonville and points nearby crowded around the heavily-laden tables of food in the station or rushed to nearby bars to celebrate.

This arrival of the iron horse did not "just happen." It was the result of efforts which began in January, 1853, when the Black River & Utica Railroad was organized. Capital did not come easily, for the Black River Canal had been opened at great expense and doubters didn't think a railroad could climb Deerfield Hill or surmount the grade between Trenton and Remsen. The engineer, Daniel C. Jenne, dodged the first problem by going around Deerfield Hill and solved the second by building a wooden trestle across the valley of the West Canada Creek. This trestle, which was 1200 feet long and about 100 feet high, took over two years to build. It stood open to the elements until 1861, when the filling in process began and the stone culvert 300 feet long and 40 feet wide were started.

The railroad was opened to Trenton in January, 1855, and stages ran from that point to Boonville. Most of the tracks had been laid, but the pesky trestle had not been completed. When it was finally ready, engineers and stockholders watched with bated breaths while inspectors ran a train over it at twenty miles an hour before putting their seal of approval on it. Much of the railroad was built in sections in charge of local contractors. A shanty town rose a few miles above Remsen to house Irish immigrants who were imported to serve as laborers.

Fuel for the locomotives was supplied chiefly by farmers who spent their winters cutting wood and drawing it to the fueling stations, the most important one being below Alder Creek station.

The railroad served its purpose. Remsen, with its dairy products, became the chief freight station. Prospect became the "jumping off place to the Adirondacks." And Trenton Falls bolstered its position as a rival to Niagara.

THE CATARACT BOYS

Boonville can celebrate a century of fire protection, for the village took over the first volunteer fire fighters, the Cataract Fire Co., No. 1, in 1856 and built a home for its hand-pumper, which was affectionately known as "The Old Tub."

The Cataract Boys loved their pumper and showed to advantage in contests against all rivals north of Utica. They went to that city in 1858 as the guests of Neptune No. 5, the top-ranking company of the area, and participated in the torch-light parade which commemorated the laying of the Atlantic Cable.

The Cataract Boys, wishing to repay the courtesy, invited the Neptune Boys to Boonville the following March for an afternoon of parading and general festivities. They suggested that the Utica outfit bring its famous pumper and engage the Cataract No. 1 in a water-throwing duel on the village park.

The Utica firemen responded enthusiastically, for they liked nothing better than to show their country cousins how a real company worked. They arrived on the Black River train with their pumper, "The Bully Machine," riding a flat car in the rear of the coaches.

In order to make a good showing, the Cataract Boys had sent to New York for fifty feet of hose made out of sole leather butts and double-rivetted. They drilled nightly, using two teams of fast, light pumpers. To measure distance, the Cataract Boys put up in the middle of the park a 165-foot pole surmounted by a gilded ball.

After entertaining the Utica firemen at a dinner at the Empire House, the Cataract Boys, keeping step to strains from the Boonville Saxhorn Band, marched with their guests to the park, where an overflow crowd awaited the contest.

Both teams made practice tries, but their best efforts were half-hearted and the streams of water did not climb half way to the pole.

Neptune No. 5 went to work. Bob Supple, their foreman, yelled, "Man the extensives!" The pumpers moved into their places at the brakes on both sides of the Bully Machine. Supple doffed his hat and smiled condescendingly at the crowd. He could well afford this gesture, for his team had never been beaten. "All ready? Steady—one-two, one-two."

The stream mounted and fell.

"Put 'er down! Put 'er down!" yelled Semple, who jumped up and down like a madman. The Bully Machine responded nobly, but its stream failed to sprinkle the gilded ball.

Foreman Jerome Hulbert lined up his Boonville firemen for their second try. One squad manned the brakes, while a relay outfit waited to spell them. Hulbert mounted the pumper and looked around. "Ready? Ready?" he asked. When the Cataract Boys nodded he cried, "Slow and easy at first. Let 'er go!"

The brakes moved up and down like clockwork, at a stroke of forty to the minute. The specially-made hose held true. Hulbert speeded up the rhythm. Up it went to seventy as the stream gained in height.

"Change relay!" yelled Hulbert and fresh men stepped to the brakes without missing a stroke. "Put 'er down! Down for your lives! Down! Down!" He waved his arms frantically as the beat increased to eighty and then to ninety strokes per minute.

The stream from Cataract No. 1 climbed steadily until it not only sprinkled the gilded ball but shot thirty feet above it.

"Stop brakes!" Hulbert's voice was filled with triumph.

The Cataract Boys gathered around the Old Tub, to shake hands, to slap one another on the back, to hug each other in a delirium of victory, while the partial crowd roared its approval.

The Utica outfit stood by during this demonstration. The Cataract Boys had shot a stream into the air that was higher than any the famous Neptune had ever achieved, but the city boys were game for another try.

Try they did, once, twice, three times. Length after length of hose burst, sending ill-directed sprays over the spectators, but the stream from the Neptune never reached the gilded ball. Crestfallen and glum, the Utica firemen reluctantly conceded victory to the home-towners, who took away some of the sting of defeat by escorting their vanquished foes to the train.

When the Cataract Boys had finished washing and polishing The Old Tub and had put it away for the night, one Irish fireman spoke for them all when he slapped the pumper affectionately and sighed, "Old gal, how I love ye."

66

A TANNERY FOR A HORSE

A collection of photographs taken by the late Frank G. Lankton over fifty years ago reveals the activities of one small village of that era. Lankton, who was a native of Gravesville, took innumerable pictures of his village. They show that Gravesville, instead of being the off-the-highway village it is today, was a thriving, self-sufficient place.

The name of the village has nothing to do with the large cemetery which overlooks it. In 1800 a Vermont Yankee named William Graves rode up the West Canada Valley and stopped for the night near Mill Brook. He entered into conversation with Major Geer, a tanner who had put up a small building four or five years earlier and was tired of his investment. Graves had no money, but Major Geer simply could not take his eyes off the Vermonter's horse, saddle and harness. At the end of the evening's talk, Geer departed with the horse and his accoutrements and Graves took over the tannery.

Industries began to spring up at Graves Hollow, as the place was soon called. With tumbling Mill Brook furnishing water power, John Burr put up a sawmill in the upper part of the village. It was soon joined by a gristmill operated by the father of Colonel J. E. Hinman, one-time mayor of Utica. When the gristmill burned in 1826, Graves erected a new mill at the cost of nearly $3,000, a stupendous sum for those days. It operated for nearly a century and remained a picturesque ruin until a few years ago.

Other industries sprang up along Mill Brook and in the village. One of the two carding mills still stands aloof from the highway near the Methodist Church. A trip-hammer shop thrived for several years and was replaced by a distillery which also had its period of prosperity. Another unique industry was a cow-bell factory.

By 1878 Gravesville boasted a gristmill, a scale-board factory, a blacksmith and wagon shop, a carding and cloth dressing mill, a schoolhouse, a general store, two churches, a machine shop, a cheese-box factory and an undertaking establishment. The post office, established in 1845, is still in operation, though the village is one of the smallest in Herkimer County.

The village had two churches, the wooden Methodist Church and the brick Universalist Church. The latter was the pet of William Graves, the father of the village, who donated the lot and $1000 toward the construction of the church, which was dedicated in 1847. After the Universalists gave up, the building served as the village school for many years and is now owned by the grange.

It is hard to realize that the West Canada Valley was without canal or railroad until 1893, but such was the case, except for a narrow-gauge road which ran from Herkimer to Poland. When the Adirondack & St. Lawrence Railroad was put through in that year, it was an event worth recording. Gravesville, with his rolling terrain, offered a real obstacle to the engineers. Mill Brook was spanned by a high trestle which took considerable skill to construct and early trains ran "on stilts" over a wooden trestle below the village. Gravesville added a milk plant to its industries and prepared for a brilliant future.

The railroad, instead of increasing industry in Gravesville, brought in outside competition which was better equipped to carry on the same activities. One by one, the tiny factories which had supplied the needs of the villagers closed, and at long last the railroad was abandoned. And, a few years ago, Gravesville found itself completely isolated when the new highway from Barneveld to Poland cut it off. It seems destined to live a quiet, sleepy life beside Mill Brook, which once turned the wheels of its varied industries.

Mr. Lankton's pictures recreate the Gravesville of a busier day. There are excellent shots of the Graves gristmill perched high above the falls, the village streets with their lines of shade trees, the two carding mills, the village store, and several of the Mohawk and Malone Railroad, including one of the first train crossing the chasm bridge at Trenton Falls.

They illustrate life as it existed in one small village over a half century ago, before improvements in communication and centralization of industry carried business from the villages to the cities.

HINCKLEY OF HINCKLEY

The Hinckleys migrated in 1797 from Pomfret, Connecticut, to the town of Russia, where Gardner Hinckley was born nine years later. His father, a prosperous farmer, owned large land holdings and built one of the finest homes in the area. When he died, Gardner, then fourteen, was put under the guidance of William Graves, the Vermonter who had traded his horse, saddle and bridle for a tannery on Mill Brook in what is now Gravesville. The boy profited from Graves' tutoring, but his health became increasingly poor as he approached manhood. Graves, deeply concerned about the young man's future, sent him to Piseco Lake to act as business agent for A. K. Morehouse, the lumberman.

The Adirondacks worked wonders with Gardner Hinckley. The climate improved his health and working for Morehouse made him see possibilities in the lumber business. In 1840 he decided to erect a sawmill of his own on the West Canada Creek at Wilmurt. The mill was completed and it ran successfully for several years.

Gardner Hinckley had greater plans. The Wilmurt mill lay too far from Herkimer and Utica, so he decided to build another mill on the West Canada Creek three miles above Prospect Falls. To increase his capital he entered into a partnership with Theodore P. Ballou of Utica. He called in James Walters, a graduate of Fairfield Academy and a carpenter and millwright on his own. Hinckley had heard about a new type of mill using gang saws. He sent Walters and Mr. Broadwell, his man in charge, to Painted Post, Corning and down into Pennsylvania to study this new type of sawmill.

Work started in October. Broadwell and Walters were in a constant state of disagreement. Furthermore, winter came early, and on the 22nd of December a foot of snow fell and the sub-zero temperature froze the hands and ears of the workmen. The framework was finished under frigid conditions and the wheels were put down in mid-winter. The mill went into operation with one set of saws in early June. By fall both sets of saws were operating. The mill had two sets of saws, one on each side of the mill, with gang-saws in the middle, all run with the old-style flutterwheel. It was the first gang-sawmill constructed in Northern New York with the exception of one on the Hudson River headwaters near Fort Edward.

Gardner Hinckley, the lumber baron, built his home on the east bank of the creek near the mill and also threw a bridge across the stream. A flourishing and prosperous community called Gang Mills sprang up on both sides of the creek, a roaring lumbering village that provided headlines for the newspapers on numerous occasions. To supply the needs of the increasing population, Hinckley built a two story store, 80 x 40 feet. This emporium, called the Hinckley Mercantile, carried the most amazing collection of goods found north of Utica.

The Civil War brought a temporary halt to Hinckley's activities. In 1862 business was suspended except for running the planing machines. Hinckley spent his time and capital investigating and purchasing land holdings in the Middle West. There was such a demand for lumber in late 1864 that Walters went to Canada to try to enlist help to cut logs, but the Canadians were leery about coming for fear that they would be pressed into military service. The mill was reopened with old men and boys operating it.

Gardner Hinckley became the father of a village. All life in Gang Mills centered around him and his family. Most of the people worked for him and traded at his store. He had a system of issuing credit slips to the men instead of money, so that they could not drink up all of their earnings at nearby bars. They would present these slips and sign them; then the recipient would turn them over to Hinckley, who would verify them and pay the bills. He must have received quite a shock one day when one of his slips came in from a brothel in Utica. No one has recorded the deathless prose he used to tell off the lumberman who used it.

Hinckley, a straight-laced Methodist, was a tee-totaler who preached temperance to his employees without results. In politics he was a staunch Democrat, but shifted to the Republican party when it was organized in 1856. He acted as supervisor for the town of Wilmurt from 1844 to 1853 and served as Herkimer County member of the State Assembly from his district in 1853 and 1854. In 1891, sixteen years after the death of its founder, the name of the logging village was changed officially from Gang Mills to Hinckley.

Part V

THE DRUMS ROLL

LINCOLN'S FIRST PORTRAIT

When the new Republican party nominated Abraham Lincoln for President in 1860, it discovered that the frontier lawyer had never sat for a portrait, so there was no good likeness which could be used for campaign purposes. A hurry call was sent for the leading portrait painter of the day to come to Springfield, Illinois, as quickly as possible and paint a picture of the candidate.

The call arrived at Trenton Falls, where Thomas Hicks was spending the summer at Thornwood, his home on the east bank of the West Canada Creek. Hicks packed his paints, brushes and bag and took a train to Springfield, where the gangling Lincoln sat for a portrait which is one of the few which show the Great Emancipator minus a beard, for he did not grow that familiar decoration until he went East to make his Cooper Union speech.

Thomas Hicks, the artist, had a career which reads like a movie scenario. By the time he was fifteen, he had built up a reputation as a portrait painter but he was not satisfied. After completing studies at the leading art schools of New York and Philadelphia, he sailed for Europe. where he spent four years studying art and visiting the famous galleries of England, France and Italy. He lived in Rome for two years, where he was part of the colony which contained, among others, the famous writers, Margaret Fuller and George William Curtis. One night, while attending a carnival, he was stabbed by an unknown assassin and dangerously wounded.

He returned to New York and immediately took rank among the foremost painters of his day. Among famous people who sat for him were William Cullen Bryant, Henry Wadsworth Longfellow, Washington Irving and William H. Seward. His favorite subject was Edwin Booth, the Shakespearian actor. The artist's portrait of Booth as Iago was considered one of his finest achievements.

Hicks' career nearly came to an end again in 1853, when a New Haven Railroad train went through a drawbridge at South Norwalk, Connecticut. He and Miss Angeline King, who was to become his bride, were riding in the first coach, which dropped into the river. Hicks found himself crushed under the partially fallen roof of the car and surrounded by a choking atmosphere. The darkened car began to

73

fill with water. He searched frantically for Miss King until the water rose to his chin. He climbed to the top of the car, where he found his fiancee, who had been projected through the broken roof. She was bleeding from a wound on her face. They were taken ashore in a boat, badly frightened but not seriously injured, though 46 people lost their lives in the wreck.

Hicks visited Moore's Hotel at Trenton Falls and was much impressed by the natural beauty of the creek, so he bought a plot of land on the east bank about a quarter of a mile below High Falls and built a combination home and studio which he called Thornwood. Here he devoted his summers to the study of nature. The landscapes he brought back to New York with him each fall amazed artists who had considered him only as a portrait painter. He also used natives as subjects. It is said that a Hicks painting of a fisherman hung for years in the office of Moore's Hotel. The subject was an old Welshman who caught trout from the creek to supply the hotel table. His name was Pritchard, but he was known for miles around as The Kingfisher.

Bayard Taylor, writer and lecturer, visited Trenton Falls shortly after Hicks had returned from Springfield, Illinois, in 1861. He took a room at the lower hotel and immediately set out in search of his friend Hicks. He found that Michael Moore, Hicks and a large party were planning a torch-light visit to the chasm, so he joined them.

"We started a little after nine o'clock," he wrote, "taking the path which leads through the forest to the top of the High Fall. The straggling procession, at least two hundred yards long, with its line of brilliant lights, winding through the dense shadows of the wood, produced a magical effect. Gray trunks and hanging boughs flashed out for a moment in golden lustre against the darkness, and then as suddenly vanished; red shawls glimmered splendidly through the dusky green; white dresses danced in and out of the gaps of moonlight with an elfish motion, and a confusion of shouts and laughter rang through the echoing hollows."

Thomas Hicks is remembered as a slightly-built, gray-haired and gray-bearded man who, along with his large but beautiful wife, made many friends at Trenton Falls. Thornwood passed into the hands of the Adams family, who still come each summer to what is one of the most beautiful spots along the West Canada Creek.

THE CONKLING RIFLES

The Adirondack foothills once had a regiment all their own, the 97th New York Volunteers, which fought throughout the Civil War with conspicuous bravery and countless losses in personnel.

On September 23, 1861, Governor Morgan of New York authorized Charles Wheelock, a farmer and produce dealer in Boonville, to establish a depot in that village as soon as eight companies of 32 men each had been mustered in. The foothills responded nobly, 300 men being enlisted in less than two weeks from Oneida, Lewis and Herkimer Counties.

The military encampment was located at the southern entrance to the village. The barracks, a canal warehouse owned by Peter P. Post, was fitted up with bunks and one wing was made into a mess hall which could seat 300 to 400 men. Three Boonville merchants took over the task of feeding the regiment at 30 cents per man per day. The official name of the camp was Camp Rathbone.

Drilling was done on what is now Erwin Park, and, despite the severity of the winter, the regiment was whipped into shape before spring. The soldiers, chiefly farmers, mechanics and woodsmen, were healthy, rugged men. They enjoyed sports, so ball games and feats of skill became common events at Camp Rathbone. Strange to relate, an epidemic of measles caused the regiment considerable trouble. Sixty men were taken sick and three died.

As the regiment grew in size, it had need for two things, a stand of colors and a nickname. The first need was supplied by the ladies of Boonville, who held a Ladies' Fair in December and raised money to buy a flag, which was presented to the regiment in front of Hulbert's Hotel two days before Christmas by Hon. Richard Hulbert, Boonville's official speech-maker. Colonel Wheelock accepted the gift for the regiment.

Names for the regiment began to pour in—The Black River Riflemen, The Boonville Regiment, The Spinner and Conkling Rifles. At the time Roscoe Conkling was an influential United States Senator from Utica and it was after him that the 97th New York Volunteers were dubbed The Conkling Rifles, a name which they bore with distinction.

75

The Conkling Rifles were officially mustered into the service of the United States on February 15, 1862. Of the 918 men, 401 were from Oneida County, 253 from Herkimer County and 122 from Lewis County. It was truly a foothills regiment.

News came through that the regiment would leave Boonville on the 12th of March. Friends and relatives sought every opportunity to be with the soldiers. And the volunteers themselves, bored by the long winter, which had been comparatively inactive despite the drills and parades, began to kick over the traces. Being under military law, they flouted the authority of the civil officers. A squad from the barracks marched through the village in military order, broke into the store of Warren Hunt & Co., rolled out casks of liquor and other liquids and emptied them in the street. Another group evidently had something against Adams' bowling alley and billiard parlor, for they made that establishment a shambles before retiring to the barracks.

At eight o'clock on Wednesday morning, March 12th, the regiment paraded in front of Hulbert's Hotel. Colonel Wheelock received "an elegant sword," after which the troops climbed into the eighteen car train which awaited them at the Black River depot, then located in the center of the village. Most of the men were content to ride in the cars, but one Irish sergeant from Boonville evidently chose to view the countryside from atop a car, for which curiosity he was rewarded by getting knocked out by an overhead crossing en route to Utica.

Boonville took the departure of the regiment in stride. "With few exceptions," wrote the *Herald*, "their behavior has been worthy of all praise. We shall expect to hear a good account of this regiment if it has ever a chance to face the foe."

The Conkling Rifles faced the foe many times, at Gettysburg, at Antietam, at Chancellorsville and in other important engagements. They were present when Lee surrendered at Appomattox Court House. When the regiment was mustered out, it consisted of 322 men, only 63 of whom had left Boonville three years earlier with the cheers of the people ringing in their ears.

COLONEL WHEELOCK'S AUCTION

Colonel Charles Wheelock of Boonville, commanding officer of the Conkling Rifles, was a florid, blue-eyed man of fifty who tipped the scales at 240 pounds. His weight consisted of bone and muscle, for he had been a farmer all his life. His respect for the common soldier was proverbial, and the men under his command considered him the father of the regiment.

The colonel, who had been captured on the second day of the Battle of Gettysburg and had escaped after a series of adventures, returned to his regiment about Christmas time, 1863. Christmas packages from home were pouring into the regimental camp near the Rapahannock River in Virginia. When all the packages had been delivered and general happiness prevailed in camp, the captain of Company D came to Wheelock with a small package and a letter. They were addressed to a young draftee from Auburn who had been with the regiment only since late July. Neither the letter nor the package could be delivered, for the young man of 24 had died at the Division Hospital a few days before Christmas. The captain told Wheelock that the soldier had left behind a destitute family. The captain thought that homesickness had contributed to the young man's death.

Wheelock sighed deeply and motioned for the captain to open the package. He personally did not feel up to it.

The box contained a small fruit cake, a pair of suspenders, a skein of thread and a paper of needles.

Wheelock got little sleep that night, for he could not drive from his thoughts the recurring picture of a frail farm wife trying to lull her children to sleep while her mind lay far away with a husband from whom she would never receive another letter. By dawn, he had made up his mind what should be done and only he, the commander of the regiment, could do it.

After morning dress parade, Colonel Charles Wheelock boosted his bulky frame to the top of a stump and signalled the men that he wished to address them.

"You all know we lost one of our comrades a few days ago," he said. "I have here a letter from his wife and the Christmas package she sent him." He read aloud the letter to show the men the dire straits in which the widow found herself. "Boys," he continued, "we don't know how soon our families may be in the same fix. This woman seems like a true wife and mother. I propose that we do a little to smooth over the bad tidings I must send her."

Taking a knife from his pocket, the colonel cut the fruit cake into forty pieces. "These pieces sell for fifty cents each," he cried, "but I shall go better and give double for mine. Who wants them?"

A rush of soldiers nearly upended Wheelock, but he disposed of the pieces in a matter of minutes.

He held up the pair of suspenders. "How much am I offered?"

"Fifty cents."

The colonel, like a true auctioneer, looked insulted. "Who'll give me a dollar?" He kept the bids rising until the suspenders went for five dollars.

"Put 'em up again," said the buyer. "I got a pair."

Cheers followed this offer, and the suspenders were put up again and again until they brought nineteen dollars.

The skein of thread was divided and brought three dollars.

Wheelock, having gotten over forty dollars from the soldiers, turned to the officers and held up the small paper of needles. "These needles sell to officers for a dollar each," he announced, using a tone of command. He got no refusals.

The auction had brought $79.50. At its close, the colonel said, "Up in Boonville the auctioneer usually chips in, so I'll put in enough to make the widow's purse one hundred dollars."

SEWARD AND THE DIPLOMATS

The most important political event to take place in the Adirondack foothills occurred at Moore's Hotel in Trenton Falls on August 18, 1863. The Civil War had reached a crisis. The Confederate advance had been but temporarily halted at Gettysburg in July, and the Southern states were pressing for recognition by powerful European countries. As a countermove, Secretary of State William H. Seward, whose home was in Auburn, invited a group of diplomats to accompany him on a tour of New York, his purpose being to exhibit the vast industrial and agricultural resources of the North and to prove that the South could not match them in a long war.

Seward's party arrived in Utica at 2:50 p.m. and took the afternoon Black River train to Trenton Falls. Prominent in the party was Lord Lyons, the British Foreign Minister, the man Seward wished most to impress, for England, with her dependency on Southern cotton, inclined toward the Confederacy. The *Utica Morning Herald* found Lyons "a good national specimen, hale and solid, with a plump face and physique, and the former not remarkably expressive." Of the group, M. Mercier, the French Foreign Minister, made the best impression. The paper referred to him as "the Frenchiest of Frenchmen—enthusiastic, polite, talkative, demonstrative, quick-tempered. He is tall, dark-eyed, dark-whiskered, and accompanies his broken English with many gestures. He made a number of graceful bows to the crowd as the Black River train moved off, and was the only one in the party who did so."

In the party were representatives from Prussia, Nicaragua, Spain, Russia, the Hanseatic League, Italy, Sweden and Chile. Michael Moore, proprietor of the famous hotel, welcomed the diplomats and served one of his best dinners. One wishes that the conversation which followed with the cigars had been carefully recorded but, unfortunately, the events of the day, which was probably one of informal discussions, have become bound up with legend.

The most impressive tale insists that immediately after dinner, while the cigar smoke was thick, a messenger rushed up to Seward with a telegram from President Lincoln, stating that the European situation was more critical than ever. Seward is said to have shown relief when one of the diplomats declared, "We are in agreement. We agree that the Confederacy is beaten. I suggest that we advise our governments that your country is in excellent economic condition. You have shown us the prosperity, power and strength of the Union. When the people at home are busy and happy—then that people's army will be successful in the field."

Taken at face value, the story has a few flaws. The New York and Utica papers of the day mention nothing of that nature taking place at Trenton Falls, though reporters must have been present. Furthermore, telegraph service had not been established to Trenton Falls. If a message came through at all, which is doubtful, it must have been carried by special messenger from Utica.

If anything of world-shaking importance happened at Trenton Falls on that afternoon, the State Department records fail to reveal it, for the Chief of the Foreign Affairs Section of the National Archives writes: "We regret to inform you that an examination of the index of correspondence to and from the Department of State failed to reveal any reference to Secretary Seward's trip to Trenton Falls in August, 1863."

The visit to Trenton Falls and whatever conversations took place at Moore's Hotel were part of a tour which surely had significance, for the South did not gain recognition from Great Britain or from any of the other European powers.

After dinner, most of the diplomats made the tour of the Trenton Falls chasm. A Utica photographer, W. J. Baker, had not been caught napping. He grouped Seward and the diplomats on the flat rock below High Falls and took two different shots of them and thus captured the most important group photographs ever to be taken in the Adirondack foothills. They stand as a permanent record of the visit, along with the signatures of the diplomats in the register of Moore's Hotel, now in the Oneida Historical Society in Utica.

A CAPTAIN'S LETTER

Near Petersburg, Va.
Sept. 4, 1864

Dear Brother and Sister:

Sunday or at least I was told that it was by the Colonel a while ago at Headquarters. Well, it is no wonder that we don't know when Sunday comes as it is all the same to us Sunday and Monday.

We hold the right of our lines resting on the Appomatox and our lines are very thin at present. I occupy with my company the same front that four companies held when we were here before, but I think that our lines are strong enough, though unless they are reinforced and we can get reinforcements about as soon as they can. Tonight Gen. Grant issued an order for all of our batteries to fire a national salute in honor of the taking of Atlanta and of course our boys fired shell into their lines and the city, which made the Jonies furious and they opened in return and we have had the warmest time imaginable. But we have our line so fixed that we don't lose many men.

Charley Jones of K Co., the same man that said he was going down with me last year, was killed today, shot through the head by a sharp-shooter. And by the way, Humphrey Hughes' boy, Thomas Jones, Roy Reese, Hugh T. Jones' boy and Eve Jeanette's boy came here and were assigned to duty in my company at dark. I had some extra guns and I gave them guns and put them on duty at once and it was rather rough on the boys to commence with but when the shelling got to be very severe I sent them into a bomb proof out of the way. You can tell Eve's mother that I gave him his drum back again. I shall make him a drummer again.

I am detailed on General Court Martial at Division Headquarters. The Court organized today. I don't know how long it will last. It may last several weeks. I have to sit from 10 A.M. to 3 P.M. and that is my day's work. We are trying one of our captains, a late appointment promoted for bravery and now I suppose will be dismissed from the service for drunkenness. Too bad that good men will throw themselves away in that manner. If he was dismissed for kicking old Ben's backsides or knocking somebody down or anything else

81

but drunkenness on duty or cowardice, I would not care so much. He is a good officer, takes good care of his men, and is brave, but he went out to the front to relieve me one night in charge of 135 men and the aide on our brigadier's staff noticed that he was drunk and sent him into camp in arrest and it was the end of him and an extra night's duty for me.

Well, Eve tells me that Remsen and Trenton are out of the draft, that Doc Crane has got Trenton out of the draft again. I like to see it. I don't care how the plague it is done or whether the men are black, white, old or young, deaf, dumb or blind; they are all good enough and they will fill up the calls and that is all that I want. Only this, I want all men for this regiment to be one year men, so that I can get home with the regiment I shall muster again one of these days for three years, and if we get many three year men it will keep up the organization and they will keep me with them.

I refused the captaincy of one company on account of muster, but I made up my mind that I might as well take it and the colonel was quite anxious and this is a good company, so I finally told him that I would be captain of Company D and I was notified that it was coming soon and I suppose that some of these days I shall be captain of Company D. It is a splendid company, a great many gentlemanly good men in it, first rate sergeants and I have got one good lieutenant. My first lieutenant is to be B. T. Miller of Utica. His father keeps a fruit and grocery store on Bleecker Street alongside of T. Thomas. He is in Washington with a broken leg received at Cold Harbor.

I must close for the present. It is getting late and my candle is about gone and it is the last one and I must try to get some sleep or I can't keep awake tomorrow at the court.

Give my love to all the folks and accept the same yourself. There is good news from Atlanta and Mobile. That is one consolation. I wish there was more of it.

from your brother,

John.

NOTE: The writer of this letter, Captain John T. Thomas of the 117th New York Volunteers, did not get home to raise a new regiment. He was killed at Fort Fisher, North Carolina, on Sunday, January 15, 1865.

GRANT COMES TO TOWN

The first of August, 1872, was a gala occasion for people in the Adirondack foothills, for on that day President Ulysses S. Grant paid a visit to Trenton Falls. Folks in Utica, thinking he would take the morning train, crowded the station to greet him, but the Civil War hero, always shy of publicity, eluded them by driving to Trenton Falls in the company of Mrs. Grant, Lieutenant Grant, Senator Roscoe Conkling of Utica, Mrs. Conkling, Horatio Seymour, A. C. Coxe and others.

The people of South Trenton evidently got wind of the change in plans, for they rose early that morning to erect a pole on which to fly the nation's flag in honor of the President. In their haste they evidently forgot to guy the pole, and it crashed to earth shortly before the expected arrival of Grant's party. Undaunted by this catastrophe, the South Trenton folks stretched a rope across the road and hung from it the Stars and Stripes, under which Grant passed to the huzzahs of the people.

Trenton Falls, which had anticipated the President's visit for weeks, had spent much time in preparation. Crowds lined the road from the Four Corners to Moore's Hotel. At the flag-draped lower hotel, the Kuyahoora House, stood the Prospect Silver Cornet Band and a welcoming committee of the best-dressed and best-looking girls in the area.

They too were caught by surprise, for the morning train was not due for some time when the three carriages bearing the President's party rolled up to the Four Corners from an unexpected direction. The band members, who had been flirting with the good-looking girls, assembled in somewhat haphazard manner and formed into line. Playing loudly but somewhat inaccurately, they led the procession toward Moore's Hotel, where the proprietor, Michael Moore, waited to greet the distinguished guest.

General Grant, who had faced foes for over 25 years, really rode the gauntlet on his way to the hotel. Crowds of happy girls raced beside his carriage and nearly dragged him to earth in a collective effort to shake his hand. The grizzled warrior evidently breathed a sigh of relief when once safely behind the walls of the hotel.

He and his party ate dinner with the Moores and then took the famous trip up the ravine to see the falls. The party started back to Utica at six o'clock.

Grant visited Utica again in 1875 to attend the reunion of the Army of the Cumberland. Legend has him visiting Trenton Falls again on the Fourth of July, but he was eating luncheon with Governor Seymour in Deerfield at the time.

A party of veterans did visit Trenton Falls on that day, but most of the celebrities did not appear, for the banquet of the night before had left them so heavy-headed that they spent most of the glorious Fourth in bed.

Rain also was of no help as three coach-loads of guests took the morning train. The Governor's Island Band played merrily, thus elevating the spirits of the passengers. As Trenton Falls was approached, the clouds broke and the sun poured forth. The Silver Cornet Band was again on hand, this time resplendent in new uniforms, and, according to the Utica paper, "played very sweetly."

Michael Moore was ill, so his son, Robert, welcomed the guests, who started out to see the falls. Soon the air rang with the echo of *Marching through Georgia,* for the veterans chose that song to sing as they tramped along the narrow path which led through the cedar-lined ravine. They returned via the forest path, still marching to the stirring strains so reminiscent of General Sherman's triumphs rather than those of the President.

After putting away one of the famous Moore meals, they lingered at the hotel until midnight. Captain Harrison Millard sat down at Michael Moore's pipe organ and played and sang, after which toasts were given, including three cheers for the Hotel Moore.

Grant's visit was the topic of conversation around Trenton Falls for years and some folks now living can recall their grandmothers or great-grandmothers telling how they had shook hands with the President and nearly pulled him out of his carriage.

HE RODE WITH CUSTER

Algernon E. Smith of Newport lacked one month of reaching his twenty-first birthday when he helped to recruit men from Clayville and Paris and marched off to the Civil War as second lieutenant of Company G, 117th New York Volunteers. After training his men at Camp Huntington in Rome, he entrained with the regiment on August 22, 1862. He fought throughout the war and was rewarded with the commission of captain. He also served as aide-de-camp to several commanders, including Brigadier General Alfred Howe Terry.

It was under General Terry that he fought at the capture of Fort Fisher, So. Carolina, on Sunday, January 15, 1865, an attack which resulted in death and injury to many men of the 117th Regiment. Capt. Smith was invalided home with a shattered arm which remained crippled for the rest of his life.

Back in Newport he married Henrietta Bowen, the daughter of H. S. Bowen, a prominent farmer and cattle dealer, and tried to live a settled life, but the glory of war had gotten into his blood, so he re-enlisted as second lieutenant in the regular cavalry on December 5, 1868.

The Seventh Cavalry was commanded by Major General George Armstrong Custer, a heroic golden-haired man dressed in buckskin and riding the best horses money could buy. Custer had been a dashing cavalry leader during the Civil War, though his unwillingness to accept discipline had thrown consternation into the hearts of his commanding generals.

Smith was with the Seventh Cavalry nearly ten years. He fought in Kansas, Kentucky and the Indian Territory and in 1873 went with Custer on an expedition to explore the Yellowstone and Musselshell Rivers and to escort surveyors for the Northern Pacific Railroad.

When Custer was placed in command of the armies in the Department of Dakota, Smith went with him. Mrs. Custer, and possibly Mrs. Smith, lived at Fort Lincoln, an isolated post deep in the prairie. Years later, the general's widow visited Mrs. Smith and sat on the broad verandah of the Bowen home writing *Boots and Saddles,* a book of memoirs which portrays the rugged life they led at Fort Lincoln. Expeditions against Indians were frequent, friction at the fort common, and Mrs. Custer's descriptions of the blizzards in winter are often hair-raising. In short, the fort was no place for a woman.

Life at Fort Lincoln might have gone on peacefully if it had not been for unforeseen events. The Sioux were living on their reservation and most of the Indians seemed content with the arrangement. Their only complaint was the irregularity with which supplies were coming through, though the weather often provided obstacles which they should have comprehended. And Sitting Bull, a non-reservation medicine man of the Uncpapas, was continually urging them to fight the government's restrictions. To add fuel to the fire, gold had been discovered in the Black Hills and miners settling claims often came into conflict with reservation land.

General Custer, never a man of tact, was not handling matters too well, with the result that President Grant had placed him on his black list. Custer knew full well that he had to perform some feat of derring-do in order to get back into the good graces of his Commander-in-Chief.

Custer failed to comprehend the Indian attitude or their military strength. All he knew was that the Sioux were leaving the reservation and roaming at will in large bodies in Eastern Montana near the Bighorn Mountains. And when he got order to drive them back to their reservation, he did not hesitate a moment.

The Seventh United States Cavalry, twelve companies strong, rode out of Fort Lincoln on a June day in 1876 with the tawny-maned general at their head. The band played Garryowen and the women waved handkerchiefs at the departing heroes. It was the last time some of them saw their loved ones, for five companies were wiped out by Sitting Bull and the Sioux at the Battle of Little Big Horn.

From the positions of the bodies found several days after the mysterious battle, the gray horse troop which Smith commanded evidently led the charge, and that is where the man from Newport fell, along with General Custer and five companies of the Seventh Cavalry.

PART VI

FOOTHILLS CHARACTERS

THE FABULOUS DOCTOR

Visitors to the Steuben Memorial pay scant attention to the cellar-hole which stands aloof from the highway on the property east of the memorial, but the man who once lived on the site achieved a local reputation that even the Baron could not surpass.

Dr. Daniel Roberts, who came to Steuben in 1818 and died two years later, brought with him, not only the best medical training Wales could provide, but a reputation for communion and fellowship with the "Powers of Darkness." He was evidently an herb doctor, and the product he and his wife brewed in large kettles was called "Welsh Medicamentum." Patients drove many miles to be cured by his magical remedies. It is said that on summer evenings the road would be lined with rigs from Ty Coch Corners to the doctor's house.

The doctor treated all patients, regardless of their ability to pay. One woman wrote from a distance, stating that she needed his attention but had no money. The doctor told her to come. Meanwhile, supposedly unknown to him, her neighbors made up a purse to defray her expenses and to cover the doctor's fee. She came and was cured, but made no offer to pay the doctor. He said nothing, even though she forgot to thank him. She was back again in a few weeks, filled with pain. He told her that if she expected a permanent cure, she had better pay him at least a portion of the money her neighbors had donated for that purpose. She paid, was cured, and returned no more.

Dr. Roberts had a fine orchard and boys like apples. A group raided his orchard one night and were climbing a snake fence loaded with plunder when the doctor appeared at a window and so transfixed them with his eyes that each boy was caught with one leg on the fence. He kept them in this hypnotized state while he reprimanded them and told them never to steal again. They never did.

The doctor rode through the countryside on horseback, carrying his medical supplies in saddlebags. He stopped one night at an inn where the rooms were dirty and the food unpalatable. The landlord overcharged him in the morning, but the doctor paid the bill without protest. Before leaving, he walked over to the fireplace and chalked out a magic sentence on the chimney above the mantel.

A maid entered the room, read the inscription, and immediately began to dance. Her mistress soon joined her. The landlord, hearing the commotion, rushed into the room and read the writing. His feet sent him into a buck and wing. This was dangerous, for he had a bad heart and such exertion might kill him. In desperation he called for the stable-boy, warned him against reading the writing, and told him to ride poste-haste after the doctor.

The boy soon overtook Dr. Roberts and explained the situation. The doctor told him to go back and erase the writing and the dancing would stop. He added a warning for the landlord. "If that man ever charges anybody such a high price for such poor lodging and food again, tell him I will dance him to death."

The most famous story about Dr. Roberts involved the theft of a watch. One day at dusk, when the office was filled with patients, a man came up to the doctor and told him his watch had been stolen while he was in the office. The doctor ordered candles to be lighted and asked his son to bring in the iron pot that was used for steeping herbs. He placed the pot bottom-side-up under the table and had the boy bring in a rooster, which he thrust beneath the pot. He then blew out the candles, throwing the room into darkness.

"An unfortunate thing has happened," he supposedly said. "A watch had been stolen. One of you has it. Step up in turn and press your hands on the kettle. If you are innocent, the rooster will remain silent. If you are guilty, he will crow."

The patients approached the kettle one by one and returned to their places. The rooster remained silent.

The doctor lighted the candles and said, "Now hold up your hands, palms outward."

All hands but two were covered with soot. To the owner of the clean hands, Dr. Roberts said, "Only the guilty fear the crowing of the cock, which changes night to day. Give me the watch."

The guilty one handed it over.

UNCLE JAKE LEWIS

If popularity contests had been common a century ago, Uncle Jake Lewis would have won any held in Remsen hands down, for he told the best tall stories in the Adirondack foothills.

Jake came up from the Mohawk Valley in the early 1840's and bought the rambling inn now known as the Hotel Remsen. He established himself immediately as the genial host, not only to Remsen folks, but to travellers who used his inn as a stopping-place on the stage-coach route from Utica to Watertown.

Meals were hearty at Jake's place and mine host was a capable trencherman. He had been a blacksmith in his youth, but his body had taken on a roly-poly appearance with increasing age. He liked nothing better than to drop into a chair, brace his stocky legs against the railing of his front porch and spin yarns. His gray eyes would twinkle as a whopper rolled from his lips and his belly would bounce up and down with the laughter which followed each story.

Uncle Jake, by his own admission, had spent a most unusual boyhood in the Mohawk Valley, where winters were severe. He would recall the morning he and his brother got up to find that the night's snowfall had covered all but the tops of the tallest trees. And there was that remarkable cold snap which had come so suddenly in the night that frogs which had been peeping out of warm ponds the day before had been caught with their heads above the solid ice and Jake and his brother had spent the following morning kicking the heads off.

Summers were also busy seasons for Jake, who was capable of binding grain so fast that he could toss a bundle into the air and bind a second one before the first touched the ground. He also lived dangerously. On one occasion a vicious bull took after him. Jake, the swiftest runner in the Mohawk Valley, was caught off guard and soon found himself about to be tossed over an eight-rail fence on the horns of the furious beast. Jake was a man of resource, even in his youth. At the last split second he grasped the limb of an apple tree and swung himself up, while the frustrated bull could only stamp and roar at him.

Uncle Jake could do anything better than anyone else. His horses were always the strongest, his steers could draw heavier loads, his cows gave the richest milk, his barn was the largest and his house the most comfortable in Remsen. Even his fireplace would outdraw any other chimney in the village. Jake had a story to support his contention. One morning a stranger came into his bar-room with a dog trailing at his heels. While Jake and the stranger talked, the dog went through some strange antics, for, despite its best efforts, the animal was being drawn toward the fireplace. Finally, with paws braced and eyes bulging, the hapless animal was caught by the draught, slid into the fireplace and disappeared up the chimney. Its yelps could be heard for a few minutes, but Jake never told what became of the dog.

Uncle Jake's best stories compared with those of Baron Munchausen, and some Remsen folks suspected that the innkeeper had a copy of that famous liar's book hidden somewhere on the premises.

Jake's outstanding yarn could have been taken from that source. Here it is, supposedly in Jake's own words:

"It was very cold that night—I should say about forty degrees below zero. The stage from Utica was two hours late. Zeke Smith was driving. Zeke's terribly proud of his horn and he blows it most of the way between Trenton and Remsen. That night we didn't even hear the sleigh drive up to the door. Zeke stormed in, his face near frizz. He threw off his muffler and coat and said, 'Damn that horn. I've been blowing on it all the way up the hill but I couldn't get nary a toot out of it.' He hung it up beside his coat and began to eat.

"Everybody crowded around him to get the news, for Zeke knew more about happenings in the world than any man north of Utica. All of a sudden, without any warning, that blooming horn began to toot, one toot for every breath Zeke had blowed into it all the way from Trenton to Remsen. Zeke rushed over and grabbed the horn. It let out one more toot. I'll be damned if the toots weren't all frizz up in the horn and when the heat thawed 'em every toot came out. And it's a true story, so help me God."

Uncle Jake retired after thirty years of inn-keeping in Remsen and died a few years later. No man was missed more and his yarns made good retelling on the streets of the village for many years after his passing.

MAJOR SAM DUSTIN

About a century ago, Major Sam Dustin and his horse were familiar sights on the streets of Remsen. Dustin was a stockily-built, round-shouldered old fellow with ruddy cheeks, sparkling eyes, a shock of white hair and an infectious smile. He had once been a prosperous farmer up near Boonville but, according to village gossip, he had frittered away his birthright by being too congenial in taverns for miles around. In his old age, he made a meagre living by selling ointment from house to house.

Folks liked to see Major Sam drive up, for he possessed a fund of gossip and snappy stories and had a way of chuckling in his throat which brought about laughter in others. Many of his yarns dealt with the days of General Training, when he, as major of the militia, had put the yokels through their paces on the village parade ground. Others he had gathered at taverns from Remsen to Boonville.

Major Sam used to like to tell how he lived in a church, and the truth is that the building in which he made his home had been moved down to Remsen from the Steuben hills, where it had once served as a Welsh chapel.

The Major's clothes were those of another day and featured a tall silk hat which he wore summer and winter. In cold weather, he wore a suit and overcoat which he had fashioned from the skins of animals and had tanned with the fur left on, so the old fellow on winter days looked like a white-haired Eskimo going to a full dress ball with his silk hat on his head.

Eccentric as the Major's appearance may have been, his horse attracted even more attention. Years before, a powerful stage horse broke its leg in Remsen and the stage driver wished to shoot it, but the Major pleaded for its life and won. He got the injured animal to his home, fashioned some kind of tackle and sling whereby the horse's hoof barely touched the ground, and set the leg. The Major evidently wasn't much of a veterinarian, for the animal's healed foot toed out at an angle of forty-five degrees and its ankle was big as a peck measure. Folks seeing the horse plodding along—the Major never drove it faster than a walk—wondered how the animal was able to lift the heavy mass and put it down again, but the fact remains that the horse served the Major for many years.

The boys of the village worshipped old Sam, for he was particularly clever at trapping squirrels and selling them in cages for household pets. It is said that one or two of the older boys "borrowed" the Major's horse one night and put it through its paces along the road to Alder Creek. They reported to their friends that the bulb-footed nag had plenty of speed left in its legs.

The Major made a fair living out of his ointment, which he called Dustin's Salve. He seemed happy to live alone, though he was no hermit. He often sought the conviviality of Uncle Jake Lewis and other tavern keepers, where he swapped jokes and tall tales and often sat chuckling long after the others had stopped laughing. And the Major's friends knew that the old fellow was thinking of better days, when he had money to spend in the taverns, for he would usually say in parting, "Well, they can never take the good times I've had away from me."

Toward the close of his life, the Major really faced bad times. He became too feeble to earn much of a living and sometimes asked for credit at the Remsen stores, something he had never done as a younger man. He also borrowed small sums from friends who lent the money willingly with no thought of any return.

Major Sam worried about his debts. He didn't want to die owing a soul, but he seemed destined for that fate until he unexpectedly inherited a sum of money from some distant relative.

A short time before he died, Major Sam Dustin visited all of his creditors. Though he had never kept any formal account of his debts, he paid every one of his creditors accurately, for he knew down to a penny the exact amount of his indebtedness to each.

ATWELL MARTIN

Atwell Martin of North Lake lived alone for over forty years in a home-made wigwam of boards and slabs. He had three claims to fame: his aversion to women, his enormous appetite and his tall tales.

Martin had soured on women years before he retired to the Adirondacks. As a young man in Steuben, he had fallen in love with a girl and probably would have married her, but his mother had pleaded with him to remain with his parents and take care of them. Atwell obeyed his mother and lost the girl, who had been married for years when his parents died. Atwell sold the family holdings and retreated to North Lake to get away from women once and for all.

He succeeded pretty well, too, for North Lake after the Civil War was a pretty isolated place. Lib Bronson, whose husband ran sort of a hostelry between Pony Bob Roberts' and Reed's Mill, tried to be friendly to Atwell. He liked Lib, but he wished she would stop smoking home-cured tobacco that smelled like burning rope.

Lib didn't visit Atwell often, but one day while en route to visit her husband on a logging job, night overtook her and her sister, so they dropped in on Atwell to spend the night. Without asking his permission, they began to fix up a bunk in his woodshed.

Atwell did not feel safe, so he found an old lock and locked them in with the explanation that he didn't want the neighbors to talk.

Lib, afraid that the shed might take fire in the night, tried to convince Atwell that the nearest neighbor was an old man who was deaf as a post. Atwell reminded her that the neighbor had wonderful eyesight.

He listened to her protests for a while and then asked, "Are you both women?"

"Smart chance we got to be any other way," Lib retorted.

"All right," said Martin, sliding the key under the door, "you keep the key and I'll let you out in the morning." With that chivalrous gesture, he walked away from the protesting women.

Hunters knew Atwell would eat quantities of food at any time. One party decided to outwit him. Right after a heavy breakfast of side pork and flapjacks, the cook suggested to Atwell that he could save them time on the trail by having his dinner right away. This was agreeable to the hermit, who downed another batch of side pork and flapjacks. He didn't seem quite full, so the cook suggested that they follow this meal with supper and then they wouldn't have to stop for meals that day. Atwell was amenable but the cook thought he saw a twinkle in the old fellow's eyes.

Atwell ate more at the third sitting than he had at the two previous ones, whereupon he rolled up in his blanket and prepared to fall asleep.

"I always go to bed right after supper," he announced.

The hunters, anxious for the day's pleasure, were stumped. All but the cook, who stirred up another batch of flapjacks and invited Atwell to breakfast.

The hermit climbed out of his blanket and did justice to his fourth meal before the party took to the trail.

Atwell told stories as if he believed them. His most famous yarn has been told many times but it bears repetition. It seems that Atwell was out in his dugout. Seeing a deer swimming in the lake, he shot it in the neck. The bullet went right through the deer, hit a thirty-pound salmon which was jumping for a fly, and whizzed away into the forest.

Atwell, after getting the deer and salmon into his dugout, decided to follow the trail of his bullet. He found that it had blazed trees for a mile and had punched its way through a hollow tree filled with wild honey.

While Atwell was tasting the honey, a rabbit which had killed three partridges got too curious so Atwell had to wring its neck.

After a long walk, he found the bullet imbedded in the bark of a tree which contained a nest of the fattest coons he had ever seen.

On his way back with the coons, he knocked off a bear and her cub who were nosing around the bee tree. His bag with one bullet consisted of a deer, a salmon, a supply of honey, a rabbit, three partridges, a nest of coons and a bear and her cub. Not a bad day's work, even for the fabulous Atwell Martin.

KETTLE JONES

Owen Jones was a stubby Welshman from the Steuben hills who spent most of his adult life trapping in the Adirondacks. He made his headquarters at Horn Lake and was known far and wide as an eccentric, somewhat cantankerous fellow who possessed the Welsh trait of sticking to his own way of thinking at all costs.

Somewhere along the way, Jones had picked up the nickname of Kettle. To the Welsh in the Adirondack foothills, such names were commonly used to distinguish one member of a Welsh tribe from another, for the Welsh had a scarcity of given names and there might be dozens of Owen Joneses in Steuben and Remsen.

The only plausible explanation for the nickname lies in the old lye kettle in which Jones concocted from the juices of wild fruits, berries and herbs a pleasant smelling liquor which had the kick of a whole mule train.

Kettle had a trained racoon which sat at table with him at mealtime. He had trained the animal to dip bread into coffee, soup or liquor, raise it to its mouth and eat it. Kettle was not a heavy drinker and there is no record of the liquor having over-affected either him or the coon, but visitors who were invited to drink what Kettle called his "belly wash" usually saw dozens of Kettles and coons before passing out.

The trained coon entranced hunters, particularly city sports who knew it was impossible to train a coon, and Kettle received flattering offers for his pet. The Welshman usually laughed off any suggestion for parting with the coon, but as the offers grew in size he decided to make hay while the sun shone.

A hunter came along and Kettle parted with his pet to the tune of gold. Other hunters appeared, saw a coon dipping bread into Kettle's brew, and took it along. Kettle found himself in the coon business.

The bubble burst toward fall, when customers began to discover that each purchaser had returned the coon to Kettle when it had refused to perform its routine away from its trainer and that Kettle had promptly re-sold it to new purchasers. Kettle and his coon were left to eat their meals without outside interference.

In his wanderings, Kettle was constantly on the lookout for gold, for he felt sure that the precious metal could be found in the Adirondacks. On one occasion he took a few of his samples to Hamilton College for assay and said nothing about the results. He did, however, carry around with him pieces of lead which he claimed he had found during his prospecting trips.

When Kettle returned from his trip to Hamilton College, he discovered that someone had blazed a trail to his camp, so he moved down to a new camp on North Lake, where he came into contact with Atwell Martin.

Kettle was cantankerous, to be sure, but he also was a man who sought companionship, so he tried to make up to Atwell. That hermit refused to have anything to do with Kettle until he got a taste of the Welshman's belly wash. Under the influence of that fragrant brew, he was willing to listen to Kettle's plans for building a dugout they could both use on the lake in jacking deer.

The two hermits from the Steuben hills made a dugout, which they launched under the stimulus of a bottle of belly wash. They hunted together all summer and a beautiful friendship seemed to be in the making for the cantankerous Welshman and the aloof Martin.

One night in the fall, the two hermits were out on North Lake jacking deer. Atwell's lamp, tied to a jack staff in the prow of the dugout, was luring the deer to its light. Atwell guided the unwieldy dugout from the stern while Kettle sat in the waist of the boat with his musket primed.

Kettle and Atwell saw the deer at the same time. Atwell swung the dugout around into a gust of wind at the moment Kettle let fly with his musket. In an instant all was darkness, for Kettle, upset in his aim by Atwell's maneuvering of the dugout, had shot off the jack staff and Atwell's lamp had disappeared into the black water.

The two hermits sat and argued in the darkness. Kettle maintained that a blunderer like Atwell never should handle a paddle, while Martin told Kettle that anyone who couldn't shoot around a jack staff should be banned from North Lake. They got back to shore safely, but that was the end of a perfect friendship.

The next day they sawed the dugout in two and each took half. Atwell, to show his scorn of Kettle's marksmanship, set up two jack staffs on his boat and swung his new lamp between them.

DINGLE DANGLE JONES

Dingle Dangle Jones often boasted that he needed no compass to guide him through the forest. He merely dove off into the woods and, except for one occasion, reached his destination without mishap.

Dingle Dangle, like Kettle and Atwell, had been raised in Steuben, where he had been a painter and paper-hanger. Like Atwell and other hermits, the breaking off of a promising romance had driven him into the Adirondacks.

Dingle Dangle was also a hand at inventing things. On one occasion he turned out a gun-sight which he claimed brought the deer up closer to him.

He was a touchy fellow. While he and George Nash were out laying a trap-line, they shot a wildcat and dragged its carcass behind them to make a game trail. Dingle Dangle was all for dragging the smelly thing to his camp, but Nash would have no part of it. That ended the friendship.

Back in 1894, Dingle Dangle took a prospecting trip to Ice Cave Mountain at the northern end of North Lake and came back with gold. He told friends that he sent samples down to Newark, New Jersey, for assay but the experts had written that the lode would produce only twelve dollars a ton and was not worth working. Undaunted, Dingle Dangle sought for a better lode. Folks who saw his samples claimed that the gold was mixed with silver, but Dingle Dangle never let on that he had discovered anything but pure gold.

Dingle Dangle used to come out of the woods on occasion to visit friends in Steuben and Northwestern. When he left the latter village one November day loaded with supplies for a winter of trapping near his camp at Snyder Lake, his friends knew he would not put in another appearance until spring. They never worried about Dingle Dangle, though they wished he would carry a compass.

Dingle Dangle got to his camp to discover that his supply of flour was insufficient to last him through the winter. He dropped his pack-basket on the floor, opened up a package of Warnick & Brown, smoked a pipeful or two, and decided he had better go back to North Lake to pick up some flour.

Finding a scarcity of that article there, he walked on to the Adirondack League Club at Honnedaga Lake, where he got a sack of flour. After spending some time chewing the fat with the guides at Forest Lodge, he thought it wise to start back to camp, for the November sun was low in the sky and a breath of winter filled the air.

The guides, watching Dingle Dangle go, sensed that the Welshman had chosen a direction opposite to that in which Snyder Lake lay.

"Hey, Dingle Dangle," one cried, "you're heading the wrong way."

Dingle Dangle stopped and turned around. "I'll hit him when I get to the other side of the mountain," he called back. "I'll hit him all right." He waved a hand to the guides and plunged into the wilderness.

The following spring Dingle Dangle's friends in Steuben noticed that he had not put in his customary appearance. They did a little asking around, but not a soul had seen the Welshman since that November day he had left Honnedaga Lake. His friends decided to get a party together and go to Snyder Lake to see what had happened to him.

They reached the camp to find that the packbasket had never been unpacked and that only a pipeful or two of tobacco had been taken from the package of Warnick & Brown on the table. They retraced their steps to North Lake and to Forest Lodge, where the guides told how Dingle Dangle had dove headlong into the woods in a direction opposite from Snyder Lake.

For years speculation as to what had happened to Dingle Dangle ran rife in the Adirondacks. A rumor that he had been murdered gained considerable credence and fingers were pointed at a certain individual. Other guessers surmised that he had either fallen and broken a leg or had been lost in his own mine at Ice Cave Mountain. Try as they would, searching parties never found a trace of the hermit who refused to carry a compass.

UNCLE ED'S WEDDING SUIT

Uncle Ed Wilkinson used to boast that he was born in the last house in civilization, and there may be some truth in his statement, for he first saw the light of day in his grandfather's home in Nobleboro way back in 1829, when the Adirondacks beyond that place consisted of almost impenetrable wilderness.

When Ed was ten, his father pulled up stakes and moved to Duanesburg, where the family lived for six or seven years, but the call of the wild was in the Wilkinson blood, so they came back to Nobleboro, and their house became the last stopping place for those rugged individuals who wished to penetrate to Jock's Lake or Piseco.

Ed adopted the only known profession in the area, that of Adirondack guide, and for many years conducted parties of "sports" on hunting, fishing and camping trips. The exploit of which he was most proud was the shooting of the last Adirondack moose. Governor Horatio Seymour was along that day and he got credit for shooting the last moose, which rears its proud head in the Munson-Williams Institute in Utica. Ed never said too much about that trip except to remark shyly that he had shot three moose the day Seymour got his.

Uncle Ed never married. Somewhere along the line he met a girl and fell in love with her. Evidently they were thinking seriously of marriage, for Ed bought a wedding suit. Shortly before the occasion, he and the bride-to-be got into a serious disagreement and either she jilted him or he jilted her, so the marriage never came off.

Ed folded the wedding suit carefully and put it away where the moths wouldn't get at it. In his long lifetime he was never known to have worn it.

Old-time guides in some ways had careers which resembled those of modern prize-fighters. When their legs grew too stiff for long tramps in the woods, they set themselves up as tavern keepers.

John Edward Spencely Wilkinson—that was Ed's full name—put up a house in Wilmurt at that point where the road to Gray branches off to cross the West Canada Creek. Inasmuch as Ed was known and liked throughout the whole area, his place soon became a stopping place for hunters and fishermen. It had two official names, the Wilmurt

House and Hunters' Home, but to the initiated it was always Uncle Ed Wilk's place.

"By" Congdon's rigs stopped there en route from Prospect station to Mountain Home and other points in the wilderness. Sports ate one of Uncle Ed's famous meals, usually a thick slice of ham smothered with fried eggs, but on occasions a slab of venison or a mess of brook trout. They bought a few groceries at his store or chatted with the 250-pound housekeeper who was with him for years. Most of them were familiar with the brown pitcher of cold beer which he used to produce from behind the narrow counter which served as a bar.

The town of Wilmurt rewarded Uncle Ed by electing him to offices—assessor, supervisor, town clerk—and the Wilmurt post office was at his place.

Uncle Ed's hotel did not look like much—a small frame house with a rather disreputable wing. He would hardly recognize his remodelled place in the trim camp which stands on the spot today. He might think his old tavern too much dressed up. So would French Louie, Johnny Leaf and the others.

Pictures of Uncle Ed show him as a dignified gentleman with mutton-chop whiskers, once dark but later turned to white. He more closely resembled an Albany politician than a backwoodsman.

He was nearly seventy when he decided he could no longer carry on at Wilmurt. His nephew, Ed Robertson, formerly Dut Barber's prize guide, had settled in Barneveld, so Uncle Ed went there to finish out his days as near as possible to his beloved Adirondacks.

Memories flooded in like the swift waters of the West Canada Creek. Most of his old cronies had passed on, but Louie was still in circulation and might stop to pass a word or two. And when the time came for Uncle Ed to go, he made a final request of his nephew.

He asked to be buried in his wedding suit. His wish was granted and he went to his final rest clad in the suit he had bought for his scheduled wedding of some fifty years before.

Part VII

THE NORTH WOODS

JOCK'S LAKE

Jock Wright returned to his home in Norway one evening, tired and hungry. He had been away several weeks, as was his custom, roaming the northern wilderness in search of fish and game. His fare had been tea, corn meal and the rewards of his hunting and fishing. He had missed Aunt Nabby's home cooking. The beef steak sizzling on the spit over the fire made him giddy with desire. He slashed off a hunk with his hunting knife and attacked it with toothless gums. Aunt Nabby, hearing a choking sound, rushed in from an adjoining room to find her husband dead on the floor. This was in 1826, in Jock's seventy-fifth year.

Much has been written about Nat Foster, the Indian killer. Nick Stoner, cast in deathless bronze, guards the heights above Caroga Lake. But Jonathan Wright has been forgotten, though his career paralleled the lives of his more illustrious contemporaries. As a young man, Jock had seen the whites of British eyes at Bunker Hill. He later had been employed as a scout on the Canadian frontier. In 1796 he had emigrated to Norway from Hinsdale, New Hampshire, and had established himself as a man of the forest. Social life in the village never claimed him.

Uncle Jock always wore shoe packs, and his step was light and stealthy as that of the game he pursued. His outfit consisted of a pound of tea, fifty pounds of corn meal, gun, ammunition, traps and fishing tackle. Thus equipped, he would remain in the woods for weeks or months before returning to Norway laden with fish and game which he sold to the less adventurous spirits in the village.

Jock went his way alone. Since he was accustomed to communing with the silence of the forest, his speech became terse and pithy and was touched with sarcasm. Even his profanity seemed semi-religious. With each trip he plunged deeper into the Adirondack wilderness. One day he returned with a fabulous tale of a lake so clear that its bottom was never out of sight. He brought back with him speckled beauties the like of which had never been seen in Norway.

One evening about 1880 two Utica "sports" put in an appearance at Ed Wilkinson's place above Nobleboro and asked him to drive them to Jock's Lake. The stocky fellow with the handle-bar mustache who did most of the talking was Amazia Dutton Barber, who had been spending his father's money rather freely. He readily admitted that he was being exiled to get him out of trouble's way. His companion, Rouse B. Maxfield, veteran of the Conkling Rifles, who had lost one arm in the Civil War, had come along to get Dut settled.

Wilkinson probably thought his visitors crazy, but he had guided sports before, so early the next morning he hitched his team to a buckboard and jounced his guests over the rough road to the end of Jock's Lake. After helping them to get settled, he drove home wondering about a fellow who would hand him ten dollars for the trip.

Much to Ed's surprise, Dut took to the wilderness. The next summer the Forest Lodge was built and Dut began to cater to the oddest assortment of visitors ever seen in the North Woods. Democracy reigned supreme at Dut's place. Bankers might be seen playing seven-up for high stakes with lumberjacks or getting drunk with hermits. Tame bears wandered around the place. Deer came up to be fed. Practical jokers kept the lodge in a continual uproar. And Dut, who charged no fees, usually enticed guests into poker games. Dut played well.

By 1887 Dut had abandoned his free policy and was charging twelve dollars a week. His lodge was always full and his guides were kept busy taking parties into the woods. At the end of each season Dut would put on a free-for-all for the natives, a day and night of drinking, card-playing and story-telling.

The Adirondack League Club took over in 1891 and changed the name of the lake and the lodge to Honnedaga. They kept Dut as manager, but his free and easy ways did not appeal to the new owners. Dut was fired and went to work on the road. His friends had left him along with his money.

Honnedaga Lake has reverted to the Indians but Jock Wright's name has been preserved in a tiny stream which crosses the road near the foot of the lake. In its ripples one can hear the crisp, sarcastic voice of the hunter saying, "This is mine." And Jock's Brook it is, even to this day.

MOUNTAIN HOME

In the years following the Civil War, most Prospect boys "drove team for By." Byron G. Congdon, a veteran of the war, had driven the famous coach-and-four which operated between Trenton Falls station on the Black River Railroad and Moore's Hotel. He later settled in Prospect, where he maintained a livery which took hunters and fishermen from Prospect station, then "the jumping off place to the Adirondacks" to North and South Lake, Ed Wilkinson's and Mountain Home. My father, who drove for By as a youngster, used to tell of the long trips back through the wilderness at night, with all the sounds of the forest ringing about his ears.

Frederick Becraft built the first place on the West Canada Creek near Morehouseville in 1850, but Mountain House did not achieve fame until 1881, when Orasmus Benajah Matteson of Utica bought it from Becraft, enlarged it, put a tower on one end, and started catering to hunters, fishermen and folks who merely wished to rest in the healthy air of the Adirondacks.

Matteson, who had been Utica's first city attorney and who owned a fine house on Genesee Street, furnished Mountain Home like a first class hotel, with thick carpets, expensive wall paper and substantial furniture. In short, Mountain Home was no camp in the woods. The table linen and silverware were of the best, and the Mattesons spared no expense in serving food "fit for a king."

Matteson was well over 70 when he opened his hotel. After his death in 1889, the job of catering to the guests devolved upon his granddaughter, Augusta Pomeroy, known far and wide as "Gussie." She was twenty-five years old at the time, unmarried, and a great favorite of the guides and guests, for she could not only fish and hunt and row a boat, but also served as a charming hostess to the rich folks who came to the hotel.

Up to this time Mountain Home had catered chiefly to invited guests. Gussie used to travel back and forth to Utica on the Grant and Hoffmeister stage. Albert Wheeler, the driver, had been a widower for several years. Morehouseville gossip says that one day in 1891 Wheeler dared Gussie to marry him. Never one to be stumped, she had him stop at the next Justice of the Peace.

107

The marriage so shocked Utica society that they cut her dead. Non-plussed by the rebuff, she and Wheeler opened up the hotel to the general public and did a flourishing business. When Wheeler died in 1902, Gussie carried on alone for two years.

This was the golden era of logging on the West Canada Creek. Lumberjacks in checkered jackets and peg-top boots were common sights around Mountain Home, and Kreuzer's Hotel a mile or so away was their rendezvous. Many of the lumberjacks were French-Canadians, and one of them, Joseph George Corriveau, took Gussie's eye. Though she possessed a fine education and he was an almost illiterate man, love conquered all and they were married.

Gussie and her new husband, commonly called Joe Caribou, operated Mountain Home until 1916, when they sold it to L. J. Helmer and went to live in a nearby cottage. Joe, an expert with horses, worked for the Wilmurt Lake Club and also served as tender for the Stillwater dam on the creek. Mountain Home was operated by the Helmers until 1923, when it burned to the ground, thus closing a fabulous era in the history of the Adirondacks.

Gussie continued with her hunting and fishing activities for several years, though she was well up in the sixties. One day, while returning from Hoffmeister, she fell and broke her hip. She walked with a limp for the rest of her life, which closed in 1931.

Joe carried on alone for three years until he ran afoul of the game laws. He was caught carrying an untagged deer out of the woods. The troopers brought him to Poland and questioned him. The old man—he was 69—acted bewildered by the new laws. He never had been able to read and the law meant nothing to him. He said he had carried out the deer to accommodate a friend.

He went back to his cottage, completely baffled by this turn of events. He brooded about the matter and did not show his face to anyone. A week later his body was found in the cottage. Either he had been shot to death or had committed suicide. Circumstances seem to point to the latter.

The Mountain Home area is still beautiful. Lying along the creek, at the foot of towering mountains, it appears like a fairyland when viewed from the highway to Piseco Lake.

HORACE GOES A FISHIN'

An aging man sat at his editorial desk in the *New York Tribune* and day-dreamed of his boyhood in New Hampshire and Vermont. He who had been the most controversial newspaper figure for over 25 years and was destined to become the unsuccessful candidate for President of the United States in 1872 sensed that he was dying of overwork and disappointment. Employees of the *Tribune* could hear his piping complaint, "I'm tired. I want to go a fishin'."

O. B. Matteson of Mountain Home, aware of Horace Greeley's wish, invited the famous editor to spend a few days at Wilmurt Lake, "the jewel of finest water encrusted in the crown of the Adirondacks." Greeley refused reluctantly year after year, pleading pressure of business.

Late in August, 1871, Greeley and his brother-in-law, John F. Cleveland, arrived at Prospect station, where they were met, probably, by "By" Congdon, the famous liveryman of that village. They stopped at the Union Hotel either for a meal or for the night and then were driven to Morehouseville.

Matteson got his party up before sunrise. Greeley ate some boiled eggs and a bowl of fresh milk before climbing into the spring wagon which was to carry him to Wilmurt Lake. He uttered no complaint as the wagon bounced over half-buried boulders and wallowed in deep ruts and nearly stood on end in places where the climb was steep as the side of a house.

Old John French and his son, Jim, met them at the lake with a flat-bottomed scow. Greeley was in no hurry to fish. Clad in his old white overcoat, he expanded his lungs and took in long draughts of the mountain air. Once they had rowed to the French camp across the lake, the editor sat on the porch all morning, listening to the birds and watching through half-closed eyes the movements of a stag which came to the lake to drink and to swim.

By midafternoon he was ready to go a fishin'. John French brought a rod and reel, soaked a leader, and began to tie a fly to the end of it. Greeley shook his head. "No, no, Mr. French," he complained, "I've no use for that. Give me a common rod, with plenty of angle-worms for bait, and I shall be a boy again." Jim French dug the worms

109

and produced a long cane rod. As the editor sat in the stern of the scow, arrayed in his shad-bellied coat and his broad-brimmed hat, he made a picture fit for the pencil of a great artist. His mild blue eyes shone through the glasses of his gold-rimmed spectacles, and a bushing of white hair protected his throat.

John French rowed the scow halfway across the lake to a grassy island and anchored it. Greeley stripped off his coat while French baited his hook. He dropped the hook in about eighteen feet of water and within three minutes had struck a pound-and-a-half trout. Flushed with excitement, he made no attempt to play the fish, but yanked it over the gunwale into the boat. His hat fell to the bottom of the scow, where it bounced around with the struggling trout. He waved away French's offer to take the fish off the hook. He did that himself, with a look of mingled admiration and commiseration. He then picked up his hat, mopped his face with a bandanna, readjusted his spectacles and rebaited his hook.

The fish were biting madly that afternoon. Greeley caught seven trout in less than an hour, weighing over ten pounds. His shirt collar wilted and the knot of his cravat had worked around to the side of his neck. He took the seventh trout from the hook and put aside the rod. "That will do, John French," he said. "Not another fish will I catch today. I have often fished before, but never at any one time did I catch enough for a meal. Half of these speckled beauties will make any man a dinner fit for a king."

They rowed back to the camp, where the seven trout were hung up where Greeley, from his easy chair, could admire them until supper time, when they were served, brown and tasty, with steaming potatoes and fresh waffles. The whole party grouped around the editor as the stars came out, one by one, and the plaintive cry of a loon sounded from the further shore. He entertained them with his recollections until nine o'clock, when he yawned deeply and announced that he was ready to retire.

He arose at sunrise, but not to fish. He sat for a long time admiring the lake and drinking in the quiet stillness of the Adirondack wilderness. In parting he said, "John, I suppose that when the season ends, like John of old, you will be left alone in the wilderness. But bear this in mind, God and John French will not be as much isolated as Horace Greeley in the living wilderness of New York City."

THE BROWN'S TRACT ROAD

The Brown's Tract Road, probably the most uncomfortable 25 miles of riding in the United States a century ago, wandered out of Boonville, was met by another road from Port Leyden at Porter's Corners, crossed the Moose River at Moose River Settlement, and wound through the wilderness to Fulton Chain.

Before 1855, when the Black River & Utica Railroad sent its first train puffing into Boonville, trips to Otis Arnold's camp near Old Forge had been made on horseback. Arnold, who had gone into the woods in 1837, would ride into Boonville, meet his customers and guide them to his haven in the wilderness. Only the most intrepid souls made the trip, but all came back aglow with the beauty of the Adirondacks.

The railroad brought a demand for improvement of the trail to Arnold's, so the Brown's Tract Road was widened sufficiently to permit a buckboard to crowd itself between the two walls of surrounding forest. It wasn't much of a road. Between Boonville and Moose River Settlement, commonly called Lawrence's, the wheels of the buckboards often got bogged down in sand or in mud, depending upon the season of the year. After leaving Lawrence's, where Abner Lawrence served meals and gave overnight accommodations, the road staggered through ruts, tree roots and brambles to Fulton Chain.

Charlie Phelps' "Old Line" became famous for transporting hunters, fishermen and curiosity-seekers to the North Woods. His buckboards left Boonville every morning at eight and reached Lawrence's at noon; here the travellers rested and had dinner, and made the Forge House at four in the afternoon if they were lucky, for it was only on rare occasions that a driver negotiated the 10 miles of ruts and submerged trees on time.

Phelps' flexibly-constructed buckboards had floor-boards supported only at the two extremes, so that they could give when the wheels hit a rock or dropped into a mudhole. Female passengers were strapped to their seats to keep them from being hurtled into the forest at either side of the road.

A contemporary traveller wrote: "From this point (Lawrence's) the road for ten and a half miles is entirely a woods road, and this one is in every way entitled to its name. It is very rough, nay, it is about as rough as it is possible for a road to be; it runs up over great rocks, down into mud holes that appear to be bottomless."

Drivers of the "Old Line" buckboards won reputations for skill in handling horses and ability to repair damage. They also were noted for letting loose rich vocabularies when their patience became exhausted. They usually stopped at the top of Six Mile Hill, midway between Lawrence's and Fulton Chain, theoretically to rest the horses, but really to retire to a secret spring for refreshment, which consisted of a stone jug of hard liquor kept cool beneath a large rock.

A Phelp's buckboard bore out the body of Otis Arnold, the Old Forge pioneer, in 1869. Arnold, in a burst of anger, had shot and killed a guide. Filled with remorse, he gained the forgiveness of the dying man, then wandered through the forest to Nick's Lake, where he took his own life. A few years later his son, Ed, took over the management of the Forge House and Arnold's was closed forever.

Abner Lawrence also made an exit in 1875. complaining that the new tannery at Moose River Settlement brought not only too many people but too many smells. "The place is all ruinated," he is supposed to have said.

Civilization was approaching the Brown's Tract Road. A new iron bridge was thrown across the Moose River at Lawrence's and a telephone line was strung from tree to tree from Boonville to the Forge House. Repairs to this line devolved on buckboard drivers, who stopped and joined loose ends when discovered. One night, after a terrific storm, a buckboard was slogging its way through the ruts and darkness when a broken piece of wire reached out like a snake and fastened itself to a spoke of a rear wheel. The driver, knowing nothing of this sneak attack, kept on going, while the wire continued to entangle itself with hub and spokes. Suddenly, the buckboard drew up with a start, though the driver had applied no brakes. He got out, lantern in hand, and made the air blue with remarks about telephone wires which tangled themselves around the wheels of buckboards.

That same year a wooden-legged railroad was being built from Moose River Settlement to Minnehaha, a development which destined the last 10 miles of the Brown's Tract Road to oblivion. The only known compliment ever paid to it was, "It's better than no road at all."

WOODEN-LEGGED RAILROAD

Fifteen hundred persons bounced over the Brown's Tract Road to visit Fulton Chain in 1887. Garmon & Crosby, owners of the Forge House and a considerable tract of land nearby, saw the possibilities of creating a resort on the Fulton Chain of lakes and were letting no grass grow under their feet. They got together with G. H. P. Gould, the lumber magnate from Lyons Falls, and emerged with a scheme to build a railroad from Moose River Settlement to Fulton Chain.

Construction began in the spring of 1888 with great enthusiasm. The railroad was laid, much as a sidewalk would have been put down, through the forest. Woodsmen went ahead and chopped down trees for the narrow right of way, while a portable sawmill and crew followed to cut the trees into the proper lengths for the ties and rails, for the latter consisted of hardwood two-by-fours secured to the ties with six-inch wire nails. Strips of iron protected the rails against abrasion on curves, while wooden trestles, one twenty feet high, carried the railroad on stilts over depressions and ravines.

These trestles also lent the railroad its name, the "Wooden-legged Railroad" or the "Peg Leg."

William Scott de Camp, who had married one of the daughters of Lyman R. Lyon, watched the progress of the railroad from Moose River Settlement to Minnehaha. As it approached his woodlands, a right of way was requested by the railroad magnates. De Camp refused flatly, but assuaged their fears by offering the counter-proposal that they terminate the railroad at Minnehaha, while he would provide the connecting link by damming the Moose River and operating a small steamboat from Minnehaha to Fulton Chain. De Camp's chief objection to the crossing of his timberlands by railroad concerned the possible danger of conflagration caused by wood-burning locomotives. When they asked him how a wood-burning steamboat would improve the situation, he replied that there would be plenty of water on hand to douse any fires. The railroad magnates, nicely trapped, agreed to his proposal, and he spent the winter in damming the river at Minnehaha and building the *Fawn*, a double-decked side-wheeler capable of carrying passengers and freight.

113

The Moose River & Minnehaha Railroad launched its three-year career in the spring of 1889, a career which provided hectic experiences for the owners and passengers, to say nothing of considerable jollity for the newspapers. The ten foot locomotive and two coaches, a combination freight and baggage car and a passenger car, constituted a noise-making, breath-taking machine which either stalled in its tracks and had to be pushed up grades by the passengers, or rolled across the wooden trestles at a speed which caused ladies to scream and gentlemen to clutch the wooden seats and hold on for dear life. The engine occasionally ran off the track and passengers had to right it and push it along, thus adding another nickname, "The G. O. P." or "The Get out and Push."

Passengers sighed with relief at Minnehaha, where they embarked on the *Fawn*, which pursued a more sedate course up the river. Occasionally the *Fawn* would get tired of waiting and parties would have to stay over night at camps and get rowed to Fulton Chain the next morning.

On the night of October 1, 1891, Dave Charbonneau, the famous guide, having been awakened by the smell of smoke, looked out of his window at Moose River Settlement to discover that the enginehouse was a mass of flames. He gave the alarm, but the efforts of the villagers failed to put out the fire, which spread to the depot. James MacBeth, station agent and general factotum of the railroad, rushed through the smoke to rescue the company's books and papers. The depot and enginehouse were totally destroyed and the little locomotive hurt seemingly beyond recovery.

It was shipped to Pennsylvania for repairs and started out bravely the following June, but something had taken the heart out of the doughty little steed. It seemed to resent being hitched to a heavy platform car much too heavy for its strength on the grades, and the green wood fuel fed to its innards caused it to puff and kick and vent its spite by showering passengers and woodlands alike with sparks. By midsummer it quit entirely, after having gone off the road several times.

The Moose River & Minnehaha Railroad, like its predecessor, received only one compliment. "Show me the man that called this a wooden-legged railroad," wrote a tourist. "One road like this is worth a thousand buckboards."

ADIRONDACK SLAVERY

A howling blizzard struck the Adirondack foothills on Tuesday, March 10, 1892. Snow fell in almost unbelievable quantities and high winds whipped it into drifts which blocked the highways and forced villagers to cling to their firesides.

The R. W. & O. train from Utica, due in Boonville at 7:13 A.M., struggled into the station at one in the afternoon. Its passengers consisted chiefly of 100 Negro laborers from Tennessee who had arrived to work on Dr. Webb's new railroad above Moose River Settlement. The thinly-clad men were marched to the vacant Finlayson house on Post Street, where stoves were installed and an effort was made to create some degree of comfort for the hapless wanderers, for the continuing storm made the trip to Moose River impossible.

The Finlayson house became a place of curiosity. Boonville folks braved the blizzard to visit the Negroes, who remained in the village until Monday. The W. C. T. U. and other organizations conducted old-clothes drives, and the best cooks vied with one another in making cakes, pies, candies and other delicacies to lavish upon their temporary guests.

The Negroes, amazed by such generosity from white folks, would dance at the drop of a hat and sing for hours for a few coppers. And on Saturday night they entertained a packed house at the Schweinsberg Opera House with dances, songs and plantation humor. Folks passed the hat and collected twenty dollars for their entertainers.

The Negroes liked Boonville so well that they were reluctant to leave for Moose River on Monday. A few managed to elude their bosses but the majority, packed like sardines in old bob-sleighs with racks at the sides, started for Moose River. The Brown's Tract Road was blocked with drifted snow. Home-made ploughs preceded the sleighs to clear it after a fashion, but progress was slow and the Negroes got out and waded through the snow to keep their feet from freezing. Tears streamed down their cheeks and their wails of unhappiness rang against the spruces.

A week had not passed before forty returned to Boonville, complaining that they didn't get eggs, butter and coffee at the Finley and

115

Stamp camps, that the shacks were cold, and that the work was too hard and the weather unbearable.

When the bosses came to retrieve their men, Boonville folks took sides and their arguments sometimes led to fisticuffs. Poormaster Jackson set up a terrific howl and sent a bill to the contractors, who paid it under protest. To top everything, the Negroes broke into the Finlayson house, cut up the mantel and the pantry shelves for fuel and endangered the house by building a fire on the floor to keep warm.

Conditions in the railroad camps became so much a concern of newspapers and public alike that three members of the State Board of Arbitration and Mediation held inquiries in Boonville, Lowville and Utica and also made the difficult trip into the woods to inspect the camps.

Their report came out in April, at a time when stragglers were still coming from the Adirondacks with new stories. Evidence showed that the agents of the Enterprise Contract Company, in particular, had made false statements about the climate and also in reference to the cost of living and the payment of transportation.

The *Utica Daily Press,* which had been the chief agitator against the contractors, breathed a sigh of relief and wrote: "It is hardly probable that any complaints will be heard hereafter, and the 'Adirondack Slavery' will disappear more rapidly than the snow."

They proved to be poor prophets. Poormasters in all villages from Utica to Lowville were tearing their collective hair. Lowville committed 37 Negroes to the county house late in May. The poormaster's book at Remsen listed "Africans" who got help, while a collection was taken up by Holland Patent residents for a Negro with frozen feet who showed up there.

Boonville men knew the cause of the trouble. "If you had not made such fools of the Negroes," they told their wives, "they would not have expected to find cake, pie and candy in the railroad camps."

A BLACK RIVER THAW

A story is told of a traveler bold,
In the days of the Hartford coach,
In a big blanket rolled, for the weather was cold,
Here he went just as snug as a roach.
But the snow gathers deep as northward they creep,
And the snow rising higher he saw,
And the driver, he cried to the man by his side,
"We shall soon get a Black River thaw."

Then the man in the coach, lying snug as a roach,
Gently smiled, like an infant in sleep;
But the horses' slow gait never told him his fate,
In the drifts so wide and so deep,
At last came a shout and they tumbled him out,
And a sleigh was his fate then he saw;
But a man with a sigh, pointed up to the sky,
Saying, "Here comes a Black River thaw."

"Let it come!" said our man, "just as quick as it can,
For I never was fond of the snow;
Let it melt from the hills, let it run down the rills,
Then back to our coach we may go."
But the wind raised its song, and the snow sailed along,
And the cold it was piercing and raw,
And the man in the rug, from his covering snug,
Wished and prayed for the Black River thaw.

When the sleigh with its load reached the old Boonville road,
Where the drifts reared themselves mountain high,
Alder Creek on the right, buried deep out of sight,
Left a white desert plain, neath the sky.
Not a fence or a tree could the traveler see,
As he cowered close down in the straw,
And the driver he sighed, as the prospects he eyed,
"By George! Here's a Black River thaw."

117

While he spoke, lo! the team disappeared with a scream,
And the drift quickly closed overhead;
While they wildly looked back, lo! the snow hides the track,
And is drifting high over the sled.
Then the traveler bold, though decrepit and old,
Hurled that driver down in the straw,
Crying out, "Driver speak, ere my vengeance I wreak,
What d'ye mean by a Black River thaw?"

Then the old gossips say, he arose in the sleigh,
And extended his hand o'er the scene,
And he laughed and he shrieked, and the sleigh groaned and creaked,
And he said, "I will tell you what I mean:
When the north wind doth blow, and there's five feet of snow,
And the ice devils nibble and gnaw,
When the snow fills your eyes and the drifts quickly rise,
That is known as a Black River thaw."

Then the traveler arose, and he smote him with blows,
And they sank in a deathly embrace;
And none knew the spot, till the June sun was hot,
And a hunter, by chance found the place.
Here they made them a grave, where the storms loudly rave,
And this epitaph lately I saw,
"Two men lie beneath and they came by their death,
Frozen stiff in a Black River thaw."

Rev. Alonzo Teall Worden, author of this famous poem about the North Countree, was born in Prospect, April 15, 1841. He migrated to Minnesota in 1859 and served during the Civil War with a Minnesota regiment. He returned to Prospect, where he joined the Baptist Church. His first charge as a preacher was in Unadilla Forks and his longest pastorate was at Ames, where he died in 1896.

Part VIII

HORSE AND BUGGY DAYS

UP IN A BALLOON

Prospect served as the ballooning center of New York during and immediately after the Civil War, for there lived "Professor" Herman Squire, billed as "the most daring and successful aeronaut living" and his wife, Nellie Thurston, "the only female aeronaut in America." Their balloons, the *Atlantic*, the *City of Utica* and the *Lorne,* made ascensions at county fairs and holiday celebrations in all parts of the state. The Squires also performed in Canada and in 1880 they received top billing, ahead of General U. S. Grant, at the Great Northwestern Fair in Stirling, Illinois.

The Squires knew their business. Nellie, a niece of John La Mountain of Troy, a veteran of many ascensions who was finally lost on a trip from Chicago, had taken her first flight at the age of eight, while her husband became a pupil of La Mountain as a youth. In 1880, toward the close of their careers, Squire and his wife had gone up 249 times, 140 of the ascensions having been made by Nellie.

Squire, who was an excellent showman, acted as his own publicity agent. He turned out handbills on a press he had installed in his home on Academy Street. He travelled from place to place, speaking before groups of influential citizens from whom he demanded and got $500 a performance. He and Nellie kept diaries of their flights, and their long letters to the newspapers describing their harrowing adventures in the clouds made interesting reading.

At Stirling a special eight-page paper appeared. General Grant received a half column on page 5, while the first three pages contained pictures of Miss Thurston and long accounts of ascensions by her and her husband. To allay the fears of the Midwesterners, who had never seen a lady take a solo flight in a balloon, Nellie wrote: "My first visit to cloudland was made when I was eight years of age. The charm of a balloon ride for me will never diminish, nor my desire to gaze still once more upon scenery far more beautiful than the mind can conceive or the pen portray. Having been acquainted with Prof. Squire from my childhood, I have marked his undisputed skill in constructing a balloon, as well as in managing one. These facts give me implicit confidence of safety, and although I claim to be and am the only lady in America who has ever attempted to explore the upper deep unattended, I am assured that while journeying in a balloon that has been constructed under his careful supervision, I am as safe as if I were sitting in a parlor with my friends."

People gathered from far and wide to witness these ascensions. The inflation of the balloon created additional interest. Squire or his "engineer," Willett Thayer of Russia, manufactured gas on the grounds. Its ingredients consisted of a ton of vitriol, a ton of iron shavings, thirty pounds of water and sufficient lime to purify the gas. When inflated, the *Atlantic,* which contained 700 yards of balloon muslin varnished until it glistened like oiled silk, drew exclamations of pleasure from the spectators.

Nellie Thurston, pretty, vivacious and modest, became the toast of the North Country. A Utica reporter expressed himself as follows: "Our reporter believes he would die happy in the air or under the ground if he could be assured of receiving half the sympathy, or being favored with the smallest portion of the good wishes which Miss Thurston had expressed on her behalf. The little lady, dressed in a neat street costume, stepped into the circle, took her place in the basket with as much ease as if she were about to take a ride about town in her phaeton. She was the center of attraction. Every eye in the vast multitude was turned upon the lovely occupant of the basket, and the silence was unbroken until the band commenced playing. At 5:07 P.M. the great air ship, with its precious freight, rose almost directly upwards for about 500 feet. Cheer upon cheer broke forth from the crowd, and the exclamation, 'Isn't it beautiful!' was in the mouths of all."

All flights were not "beautiful." Squire, trying to make an ascension from the public square in Brockville, Ontario, had his balloon caught by a gust of wind and was left dangling in the basket from a church spire, from which precarious spot he was rescued by a daring Canadian. Nellie, taking off from Watertown, lost her bearings and let her balloon wander into the Adirondacks, where it finally came to rest in a tree at dusk. She spent the night listening to the howls of wild animals and in the morning struggled three miles on foot through undergrowth to a clearing and safety.

A GLOW IN THE NIGHT

From the Civil War to the turn of the century, grandfather's quarry at Prospect supplied limestone blocks to builders over a radius of 100 miles. For building he cut water tables, copings, pilasters, lintels and sills, also steps and decorative blocks. Bases and sockets for monuments also had to be provided, and the Welsh cemeteries north of Utica are dotted with limestone slabs fashioned by his workmen.

He also ran one of the several lime-kilns which burned incessantly along the West Canada "Crick," smudging the landscape by day and flaming like gigantic glowworms when darkness settled over the fields. In these stone fortresses wedged against the banks were calcined tons of stone, manufacturing quicklime which he sold to artisans and farmers at twenty-five cents a bushel.

Filling the kilns was an art. The circular openings in which the stone was calcined were twenty feet deep and from ten to fifteen feet in diameter. The first stones placed in the kiln formed an arch upon which the tons of broken pieces would rest. Any miscalculation in the placing of the foundation stones might result in the collapse of the whole structure, so the quarryman had to understand the importance of the arch as a supporting force.

Once filled with stone, the kiln was ready for ignition. A fire was started in the square opening on the face of the kiln. Wood was fed to the hungry flames for several days and nights by an attendant called a lime-burner, for a constant temperature had to be maintained in order to calcine the stones. When the lime had been "burned," several more days were required for it to cool sufficiently for teamsters to carry it off to the waiting artisans and farmers.

The burner's task was tiresome and lonely. Two men were assigned to the job, one working from sunrise to sunset, the other spelling him through the long night hours. These men were usually Welsh, filled with superstitions they had carried with them from their native mountains. In the shadows of the cedars often lurked Y *Tylwyth Teg* and Yr *Ellyllon,* good and evil fairies and goblins who had crossed the ocean to play jokes upon the solitary man sitting in the glow of the fire. And it is true that local pranksters played upon these beliefs to enliven the shadows with ghostly figures which dodged from cedar to cedar or broke the stillness with weird cries.

Grandfather's kiln was a gathering place for the youth of the village. Many a boy tested his strength there in a wrestling bout. Ringing were the laughs which followed a spicy anecdote. And the ancient stile provided an ideal resting place for lovers returning to the village after a corn roast or a popcorn bee enjoyed in the glow of the fire.

Yes, in grandfather's day the kilns were scenes of bustling activity. Wagons piled high with wood from the north country rolled along the creek roads. The drivers usually were French-Canadians, from whose lips profanity and song poured with equal facility. When the kilns burned out forever, the death knell of the picturesque wood-chopper also was sounded. And the cedars have thrown a green curtain across the roads which once resounded to storied jest and lusty song.

It is human to turn our eyes back upon these days and bask in the romantic glow from the kilns without taking into consideration the difficulties which grandfather and his contemporaries faced. Grandfather's account books, kept in a neat hand, are reminders of an industry which once flourished along the banks of the West Canada Creek. And the letters he received in the years following the panic of 1873 reveal the hysteria of his business partner, the pressure of his creditors and the defeatism of his debtors.

Grandfather's system of bookkeeping would not find favor today. Each charge was recorded in a daybook. When payment was made, he drew two neat crosses through the charge. And at the end of each month he listed the unpaid bills, the debit page facing the credit page. The book is living evidence of the struggle through which one small business man passed during the years following the crash of Jay Cooke and other speculators of the post Civil War era.

The results of grandfather's handiwork were once common in Norwich, Herkimer, Rome and other cities, but the work of which he probably was most proud can be seen each day in Utica. Grandfather, like most of the early Welsh, was a very religious man, and I like to feel that he often raised his eyes with pride to the stone spire which watches over Utica's busy corner, for he witnessed definite evidence that his hands had contributed to the building of a house of God.

PRESIDENT AND FIRST LADY

Sunlight pouring through the windows of Dr. Delos A. Crane's study in Holland Patent broke up the all-night card game. The elderly physician walked to the door, opened it, and picked up the morning paper.

The mayor of Buffalo, a portly, middle-aged bachelor with twinkling eyes and a heavy mustache, stretched luxuriously and tilted back in his chair. "Anything new this morning, Doc?" he asked.

"The Democrats are considering nominating you for lieutenant governor, Grover. I'd do a pack of thinking before accepting. If they offer you the nomination for governor, take it. If not, stay in Buffalo."

Grover Cleveland accepted his old friend's advice. He got the gubernatorial nomination and was elected to the office. He went on to serve two terms as President of the United States, the only boy from the Adirondack foothills ever to achieve that distinction.

Cleveland had come to Holland Patent as a boy of fifteen. His father, Rev. William Cleveland, had preached only three times at the Holland Patent Presbyterian Church when he died suddenly, leaving a wife and nine children. It is said that ten Holland Patent citizens chipped in $100 each to purchase for the destitute widow the dwelling on the main street which is still known as the Cleveland house.

Grover, who had been attending school in Clinton, gave up to go to work, and returned to the home only for short visits.

The Cleveland family grew up in Holland Patent. Four of the girls married and left the village. William N. became a Presbyterian minister who at one time preached in Forestport. Tragedy had struck the family again, for two of the boys had been lost at sea while on a voyage to the West Indies.

Rose Elizabeth, the only Cleveland girl who never married, spent her life in the family home in Holland Patent, except when she went with Grover to the governor's mansion in Albany and became First Lady at the White House between 1883 and 1887.

Washington correspondents saw her as a woman with a "slender figure and fair brown hair, which curls naturally and is worn short,

125

but not cropped, a style becoming to the contour of her head. She has a bright, self-possessed manner."

Holland Patent remembers her as a woman who defied the conventions of her time. She wore low shoes and her skirts did not reach within four inches of the ground at a time when other women lifted their long skirts from the ground scarcely far enough to show an ankle while eluding a mud puddle. Her bobbed hair caused many an eyebrow to be raised, for such a hairdo almost automatically stamped its wearer as a scarlet woman, which Miss Cleveland surely was not. Her one concession to prevailing fashion was the high-necked dress, which she persisted in wearing long after the style had gone into discard.

She engaged in many activities. She delivered historical lectures at ladies' seminaries, stumped for the prohibition movement, and wrote books for children. She particularly loved hiking, and her angular figure was a familiar sight in the fields and woods surrounding Holland Patent.

Grover paid her frequent visits. He would usually wire ahead for the local liveryman to meet him at the station, but on several occasions he missed connections and landed on foot at the Cleveland house in the middle of the night. He had many friends in the village, and liked to gather with them at the Clarendon House for social visits.

After Grover married, his visits to Holland Patent became less frequent, and his wife replaced his sister as First Lady during his second term as President. He lived on for years in Princeton, New Jersey, where his conservative ideas threw many a road block in the path of Woodrow Wilson while the latter was president of Princeton University.

Rose Elizabeth made her home in Holland Patent until the outbreak of World War I. She sailed for Italy to do war work, though she was well advanced in years. Her strength failed her and she died 3,000 miles away from Holland Patent, but that village will always remember her for her advanced ideas and for giving them the only First Lady ever to come from the Adirondack foothills.

FIVE AND DIME

When Frank W. Woolworth died in 1919 at the age of 67, he left a fortune estimated at $65,000,000. His company owned more than 1,000 stores and had erected, in 1913, what was then the world's tallest building.

The Horatio Alger story began way back in 1873, when a tall, blond youth from neighboring Great Bend dropped into Augsbury & Moore's Watertown store and asked for a job.

W. H. Moore opened up with the typical questions of the day—Do you smoke? Do you drink? When Woolworth answered in the negative, Moore went into the usual harangue about long hours, difficult work, etc. The youth from Great Bend offered no comment, so Moore fired the crusher at him. "If we take you on you'll have to do all the mean work—deliver packages, sweep, wash windows, clean spittoons and anything else which has to be done."

"What will you pay?" asked Woolworth.

"Pay?" snorted Moore. "You should pay us for teaching you the business."

"I'll work for three months for nothing if you'll guarantee me $3.50 a week for the next three months."

Moore hardly expected this answer, but he felt that the young man meant business, so he agreed.

Woolworth did not prove to be any ball of fire, but he did his work well and Moore advanced him to $6 a week after a year and a half. Woolworth might have stayed in the rut if he hadn't fallen in love with Jennie Creighton. When Moore refused an advance, he went to work for A. Bushnell & Co. for $10 a week. This firm overworked him and his health failed. He returned to Great Bend. His strength returned in the spring and he and Jennie were married, though the next dollar seemed far away.

Moore, who had been watching young Woolworth, wrote him to come back and he would pay $10 a week.

One day, while young Frank was at work, a friend who had returned from the West came in with the story of the startling success he had experienced through selling articles at five cents each. Moore pooh-poohed the idea but Woolworth pricked up his ears. He

127

talked Moore into buying $100 worth of cheap goods from New York.

It was Fair Week in Watertown. Folks found special counters at Moore's filled with tempters at five cents each. Woolworth sold out every article the first day, so Moore sent to New York for another lot, which also disappeared like magic.

Needless to say, young Woolworth thrilled with excitement. He was like the man who had come up with a better mousetrap. He wanted to set up for himself in a store which would feature five cent merchandise. Watertown wasn't large enough, so he got his father to endorse a note for $300 and persuaded Moore to trust him for an equal amount in merchandise.

The first Woolworth store opened in Utica on February 22, 1879, and closed in April. The first few days had been worldbeaters, but as the novelty wore off business declined. In later years Woolworth attributed his initial failure to two reasons; the poor location of the store and the limited amount of articles which could be sold for five cents.

He returned to Watertown to find that Moore still believed in him and in his ideas. His former employer lent him more stock so he could try again.

Woolworth went down to Lancaster, Pennsylvania, in June and opened up a new store, this time featuring goods at five cents and ten cents, the original "five and dime." He grossed $9,000 the first year. During the next few years he established stores in Scranton and Reading. He needed help, so he brought his brother Charles into the business.

Expansion was rapid. Stores seemed to spring up like mushrooms all over the country, most of them operated by old friends from Watertown. These men conducted the stores in their own names, though Woolworth had a hand in buying merchandise and in financing the various firms.

The Woolworth Company came into being in 1912, when 631 stores joined in the corporation.

Frank W. Woolworth always had a soft spot in his heart for the North Countree. Friends from Watertown often visited him in New York and received hearty welcome. The old man liked to reminisce about his youth in Great Bend or his first storekeeping days at Augsbury & Moore's in the old American House.

ACCORDING TO BIJAH

Village reporters for the *Boonville Herald* during the Gay Nineties really let themselves go in writing up news from their respective communities. They elaborated on local events, kept track of the weather, poked harmless fun at their neighbors, and engaged in witty battles with each other.

The ace of the newspaper's staff was William P. Dodge, who signed his Prospect articles BIJAH. Bill, who owned a hotel in that village, also served as clerk of the state senate in Albany. A husky, genial man, he had a host of friends, some of whom he kidded in his column. He served the *Herald* for about ten years, until his untimely death in 1900 at the age of 57.

He particularly enjoyed lampooning folks in his village who kept their fingers on everybody else's business. He dubbed his group the Committee of 47. Here is one of his comments:

"Last Monday the snow plow started in to raise the blockade on the Snow Shoe branch of the A. & St. L. railway from the junction to Hinckley. We were away from home the day they began operations, but members of our old original committee of 47 turned out in goodly numbers and superintended the job, offering advice and suggestions to the struggling crew on the snow plow, at the old rates. Matters seemed to swash along fairly well until towards night, when the committee began to suffer from cold, hunger and thirst, and were compelled to go home and rest. This movement on their part discouraged the railroad men, and they left the plow standing at the edge of the Coonradt cut, where one of the committee told a reliable citizen that the snow was 700 feet deep. This may sound rather large, but to stand by the committee has, as a rule, always been the policy of BIJAH."

Dodge put up a fountain near his hotel, and the curiosity-seekers gathered en masse to help him out, whereupon he wrote: "We take this opportunity to say to the numerous parties interested, that in the morning and evening, when we are busy, to have every wall-eyed, lop-sided, knock-kneed, superannuated, weak-spined, tallow-faced, red-nosed sucker, who hasn't even the courtesy and good breeding required in Talbot's lumber camps, to have this kind of ducks step up and ring

129

the doorbell and in a sort of terra cotta voice inquire, 'Why don't yer heve yer durned founting out here squirt as high as the ruff to ther meetin' house?' is becoming somewhat tiresome, and begins to wear the rolled plate off from the amiable disposition and Christian spirit of Bijah."

Welsh predominated in Prospect at the time, and Bijah enjoyed taking an occasional swipe at them. "They were cutting ice last Thursday on Richard Jones' pond," he wrote, "when one of the workmen discovered a lot of teeth lying on the bottom of the pond and immediately raised the cry that there must be a body somewhere in the vicinity. While they were formulating a plan to clear up a mystery, they noticed a neighbor coming with a potato hook spliced to a pole. Without saying a word, he dropped his grappling iron into the pond and brought up the teeth. Clapping them into his mouth, he was ready to talk in four languages — Welsh, English, Cymraeg and Sacsneg — and in the different languages explained to the wondering crowd that he got in an animated discussion on religion earlier in the day with Price Jones and in emphasizing strongly a particular point he blew his teeth out with such force that they slid into the opening and disappeared. One of the boys suggested that it might be a good plan to fasten them to his ear lappers until we got down to bare ground again."

He had two rivals in Mary Mitchell of Remsen, who signed her articles Burdock and Elder Clark H. Wetherbe of Holland Patent, known as Nibs. Bijah was far too clever for Nibsy, as he called Wetherbee, but Miss Mitchell often waged successful warfare with the man from Prospect. She and Dodge were good friends, and her summation of the man is probably as accurate as one can find: "The versatile and brilliant Prospect correspondent of this paper was in the village one day last week exchanging greetings with his numerous friends. Bijah, by which name he is generally known, seems at all times to be carrying full sail and a favorable breeze. He is a good steersman; at least his journey thus far leads us to conclude that he is. His perennial good humor and jocose manner of addressing friends make him popular with the people and consequently successful as a politician. As a citizen he is apparently the pulse of Prospect, his native town."

THE GYPSY'S GRAVE

Gypsy bands often travelled through the Adirondack foothills during the late nineteenth and early twentieth centuries. They camped for days on the outskirts of villages and wandered on when they had outworn their welcome. These gypsy caravans, with their spirited horses and covered wagons, added considerable color to the lives of the villagers. The bright costumes, the horsetrading and the fortune-telling often attracted visitors to the gypsy camps, while the villagers kept both hands in their pockets and locked their doors against stealthy intruders, for the gypsies, though good-hearted, usually possessed clever fingers and had their eyes open for any loot which might come their way.

A band of gypsies came annually to camp in a grove at the Roberts farm about a mile from Prospect on the middle road to Remsen. They brought along superior horses, some of the racing variety, and at one time owned a covered wagon which cost $1,800, a stupendous sum for those days. Their leader, an Irishman named Phillips, always flashed plenty of money, and it was said that he came from a wealthy New York family and merely played gypsy during the summer months.

When Phillips and his band stopped at the Roberts grove in July, 1880, his wife, Hattie, was big with child. She also was dying of consumption. She gave birth to a girl, but her strength was unequal to the ordeal.

Her passing posed a problem, both for the gypsies and for the villagers. The dead woman and her husband were Catholics, and the Prospect cemetery was at that time a Protestant graveyard. Even the potter's field contained no Catholics. Furthermore, the Welsh Calvinists of the village considered wandering gypsies a godless group of people, and it did not seem proper for the woman to be buried near their dead. No living person seems to know how the problem was solved, but a compromise was evidently reached, for Hattie Phillips was buried at the extreme eastern end of the cemetery, in a lonely spot too far away to contaminate the souls of villagers who had been interred in the graveyard. The gypsies themselves conducted the funeral service.

The band wandered on, carrying with them the baby girl. They

131

returned year after year to the Roberts grove, but they never paid any attention to the grave of Hattie Phillips, and evidently neglected to pay for the plot of ground.

There was living in Prospect a little girl who was much upset, not only by the gypsy mother's death, but by the callous attitude of her elders toward the lonely grave. She took it upon herself to be the personal caretaker of the plot at the edge of the cemetery. Each week for many summers she picked flowers from her mother's garden and carried them to the grave, where she arranged them carefully and often pondered about the lonely woman who had been buried so far from a group of wanderers who did not seem to care anything about her.

The years wore on, and the little girl grew to womanhood. She no longer put flowers on the grave, which became overgrown with weeds. Older people occasionally recounted the tale of the gypsy woman's death, but the rising generation showed no interest in the grave.

In 1910, thirty years after the death in the gypsy camp, a beautiful woman appeared in the village. She went to the graveyard but was unable to find that for which she was searching. After talking with some of the older people, she returned with a guide who located the spot where Hattie Phillips had been buried on that July day so many years before.

The strange woman, who up to this time had given no inkling of her identity, told her guide that she was the baby who had been born at the gypsy camp in the Roberts grove. She went to a stone-cutter, ordered a marker to be placed over her mother's grave, and left as mysteriously as she had appeared.

A gypsy caravan passed through Prospect last summer, the first to be seen by the villagers in many years. These gypsies were travelling in modern style, with powerful automobiles and shiny trailers. They did not linger in Prospect, but drove up along Hinckley Lake toward the Adirondacks, but their appearance brought back to old-timers memories of the sleek-coated horses and the fantastically dressed gypsies who used to come annually to the village.

BOODY'S IMAGE GALLERY

A major attraction of the horse and buggy days was Jacob W. Boody's Image Gallery, which could be reached only after a stiff climb into the Steuben hills over water-shedded roads. Puffing and wheezing horses stopped to rest on "Thank you, Ma'ams," while red-faced drivers mopped their brows with bandannas and long-skirted women readjusted hairpins which had been loosened by the bouncing buggy or two-seater.

Visitors were greeted at the summit by Jacob Boody himself, a white-whiskered old man dressed in a costume which featured a derby hat and a swallow-tailed coat. Boody was the perfect host. Everything about his manner, his voice, his smile of welcome and his dignified bearing, made each arrival his special guest. And his attractive house, reached over terraced lawns dotted with statuary, evoked little cries of happiness from the ladies.

Visitors usually brought basket lunches, which they ate at tables Boody had provided for them. He also performed little acts of courtesy, such as building a fire so they could roast corn, or lending them his long ship's telescope, so they might pick out the boats and men working on Oneida Lake, which shimmered along the horizon.

Boody was one of the most versatile men ever to live in the Adirondack foothills. He kept a good farm and raised a large family. He got along with his neighbors, though they looked askance at his multifarious activities. Visitors from the cities, however, fully appreciated him, and spent hours discussing phrenology, geology, ornithology, history, taxidermy and religion with the pleasant little man from the hills.

Though he had no professional training as a sculptor, some of the statues he carved out of native stone showed a touch of genius. He spent thirty-five years making images out of stone and his yard held an amazing collection of prominent people, Biblical scenes and family records. Though his favorite subjects were Abraham Lincoln and Grover Cleveland, he also tried his hand on Aristotle, Julius Caesar, Christopher Columbus, John Wesley, Pocahontas, Lot's wife and Baron Steuben, to mention a few. One stone, surmounted with Carry Nation's hatchet, was devoted to women's rights, and another contained the record of the Boody family.

133

His prize exhibit, however, was a mottled gray stone weighing ten tons which he had hauled to the Boody farm behind eight teams of horses. He called it "the stone of mystery" and in a prepared lecture explained to visitors the various markings on its surface.

On occasion, Boody liked to play what he called "the language of passion." His instrument was a buzz-saw and to its accompaniment he sang verses he had written.

He believed in prohibition, though he might look the other way when a party of gay young blades brought a few bottles of beer in their picnic baskets.

His home served as a museum for Indian relics, stuffed birds and animals and a bottle of alcohol containing an appendix, which he claimed he had removed from his own body with a razor.

The climax of the tour brought visitors to a wall cabinet on which was inscribed: "I am fearfully and wonderfully made. Great and marvellous are thy works."

Boody would step majestically to the cabinet, deliver a brief lecture, and press a button. The doors would spring open to reveal the skeleton of an Indian girl about ten years of age. Boody would explain that the cleavage in the skeleton's chest had been made when the girl had been killed in battle by a blow from a tomahawk.

Toward the close of his life, which ended in 1907, Boody made several phonograph records of his lectures, so his family could hear his voice long after he had passed away.

The Boody place may be reached over rough roads and through the guidance of one who knows the Steuben hills. Boody's granddaughter and her husband occupy the house with its collection, while the statuary still adorns the yard. If the town of Steuben would build a hard road to the Boody place, the museum would attract tourists from far and wide.

Part IX

THE FOOTHILLS COME OF AGE

THE RED AND BLACK.

Watertown will never forget that first week of December, 1901.
Trains began disgorging passengers by Wednesday night. The hotels
filled rapidly and by Saturday rooms were at a premium all over the
capital of the North Country. It was a colorful throng. St. Lawrence
University students poured in, wearing scarlet and brown armbands.
The delegation from Clarkson proudly displayed their green and gold.

A college football game? No, a professional contest for the
championship of Northern New York between Watertown and Ogdensburg. So keen was the rivalry that Ogdensburg arrived 1,000
strong in a special twenty-coach train.

All business stood still on Saturday. Stores and factories closed
for the day. Some companies engaged special trollies to take their
employees to Glen Park, where the contest took place. The Agricultural Insurance Company, being a trifle more conservative, sent its
workers to the park in hacks.

Glen Park, on the outskirts of the city, was the popular recreation
center of the Gay Nineties. It had a large pavilion, underground
caves, and a natural amphitheater with terraced seats for the spectators. Here the game was played and Watertown won it 23 to 0
before 5,000 screaming fans.

The team which represented Watertown was the famous Red and
Black, an aggregation which gained renown all over the state. It
was no ordinary collection of football players. College stars occupied
most of the positions, for at that time these men did not lose their
amateur standings for picking up a few loose bucks on the side. The
ace of the Red and Black backfield, Phil Draper of Troy, had been
an All-American halfback at Williams College. The line featured Fred
Metzger, a 210-pound center rush from the University of Buffalo.
Other colleges represented on the Red and Black were Purdue, Clarkson and Princeton.

Watertown backed the Red and Black to a man. When games were
played out-of-town, 1,000 spectators and the 39th Separate Company's
band went along. College teams furnished most of the opposition, for
professional teams of the caliber of the Red and Black were rare in

the North Country. Bucknell, Clarkson, Rochester, St. Lawrence and Union were played at one time or another.

The driving force behind professional football in Watertown was none other than the Mayor, James B. Wise, a progressive who built the City Hall, paved the Public Square and made innumerable improvements during his four terms in office. A self-made man who had accumulated a modest fortune, he took no salary as Mayor and put his own money into worthwhile ventures, including the Red and Black, his pet project.

Under Wise's leadership the Red and Black, loaded with college stars and with a payroll of $15,000 a year, captured the undisputed championship of Northern New York and went on to claim the national professional championship in 1903.

Players on this team's line were Nelson Longtin and George Putnam, ends; Ralph Barter and Bill Palmer, tackles; Bill Caldwell and Bill Edgehill, guards, and the enormous Metzger at center. The backfield, considered the trickiest in the country, consisted of Draper at left half, Bill Bottger at right half, Harry Mason at fullback and Ernest C. White at quarterback.

Mayor Wise, confident that his team could beat any professional outfit in the country, arranged a great tournament to be played under lights at the old Madison Square Garden in New York. The best professional teams in the East were invited to try their skill against the fabulous Red and Black.

The tournament was held just before Christmas and all of Watertown wanted to move to the metropolis for the games. The chamber of commerce, worried for fear the home folks would do their holiday shopping in the big city, vetoed the suggestion that an excursion train be run to New York, the only living evidence where the mercenary side of Watertown got the better of its local pride. Despite this rebuff, most of the Watertown sports made the trip to see the games. Whether they shopped or not doesn't seem to matter.

Two teams sailed through the tournament to the finals, Connie Mack's Philadelphia Athletics—not the baseball team—and the highly-rated Red and Black. McGillicuddy's boys put the crusher on the team from Watertown to the tune of 12 to 0. Wise is reported to have lost a cool $8,000 on the one historical attempt to put Watertown into the big league of sports.

THEY MET HEAD ON

The two single-track railroads which serve the Adirondack foot-hills may well be proud of their safety records, but during the first decade of this century they each suffered head on collisions which re-sulted in death, injury and property damage.

The first accident occurred in the spring of 1903, when the Adiron-dacks were recovering from the worst forest fire ever to strike them. On Saturday afternoon, May 9th, Mohawk and Malone train No. 650 received orders at Fulton Chain to take the siding at Nelson Lake to permit two sections of northbound No. 651 to come through. A second order followed a few minutes later: "2nd No. 651 will take siding and meet No. 650 at McKeever instead of Nelson Lake." When the fireman and the engineer read this second order, they inadver-tently held their thumbs over the "2nd" and concluded that both sections of No. 651 would take the siding at McKeever.

Their train, filled with passengers either enjoying magazines or gazing out of the windows at the charred remains of what had once been virgin forest, passed the Nelson Lake siding. Suddenly, rounding a curve straight ahead, appeared the first section of train No. 651. The horrified engineer of No. 650 slapped on the air, yelled for the fireman to jump for his life, and leaped from the cab.

The two locomotives locked horns in a crash which threw the passengers of both trains into the aisles, against the doors and even through the windows. A quick-thinking trainman opened the escape valves on the locomotives, thus preventing combustion or scalding by steam. Men rushed frantically to and fro, trying to extricate passen-gers from the rubble that had once been coaches.

A hurry call brought Dr. Wood of Old Forge, Drs. Morey and Sparks of Remsen, and Dr. G. D. Jones of Utica to the scene. They, with the aid of passengers, treated the injured. The conductor of the northbound train and the fireman and the news agent of No. 650 lost their lives, while 28 persons were seriously hurt.

At the coroner's inquest, the heart-broken engineer of No. 650 admitted that he might have covered part of the second order with his thumb. The jury cleared him of criminal negligence and ruled that the collision had been accidental.

Five years later, on the morning of July 4th, the Rome, Watertown & Ogdensburg Railroad's Clayton Flyer No. 55 arrived in Boonville two hours late. Here the conductor found instructions telling him to wait until 5:15 A.M. for freight No. 90 from the north. Though the order must have irked him, he waited. Once the Flyer hit the road, the two locomotives got up steam and raced down the long grade to make up for lost time. The passengers, asleep in their uppers and lowers, failed to notice any increase in speed.

Meanwhile, freight No. 90 had reached Lyons Falls. Its conductor received an order from the young lady who was night telegraph operator at the station. It read: "No. 55 (Passenger) will wait at Boonville until 5:55 for No. 90 (freight)."

"We can make Boonville long before that," the conductor reasoned. The engineer jumped into his cab and the fireman fed coal to the locomotive. The freight chugged out of Lyons Falls and headed for Boonville. It roared across the Sugar River and approached a section where a thickly wooded curve rose ahead.

A farmer at Denley saw the two trains approaching the curve, the Clayton Flyer from the south, the freight from the north. He raced toward the track, waving frantically with his hat for the freight to stop.

He was too late, though the two engineers, acting instinctively, tried to stop their trains. The engineer of the freight jumped at the last split second and survived with two broken arms and a cut head. The fireman and head brakeman were killed instantly. So were the engineers of the two passenger locomotives, they being buried in the debris. One fireman jumped to safety but another lost his life. A passenger who died of injuries raised the death toll to six.

Two crashes, nine lives; two people with human frailties, one an engineer who misinterpreted an order, the other a young lady who, in her haste, wrote 5:55 instead of 5:15: it all added up to the two worst head on crashes in the history of railroading in the foothills.

MAN-MADE LAKES

When the State of New York decided to build the Barge Canal, two reservoirs were needed to act, not only as feeders for the new inland waterway, but also to provide flood control for the Mohawk Valley. The sites chosen for the reservoirs were Delta, a tiny village amid rolling farms near the headwaters of the Mohawk River, and Hinckley, the roaring lumbering village on the West Canada Creek.

Delta, a triangular-shaped section named after the Greek letter D, lay south of Westernville along the line of the Black River Canal. It had been settled in 1789 and eight veterans of the American Revolution rested in its graveyard. It boasted a church, a store, a gristmill, a sawmill, a hotel and about fifty houses. Olney & Floyd's factory employed 150 people during the canning season and E. O. Coon claimed that his cheese factory was the second oldest in the United States. The surrounding countryside consisted of rich farms dating back a century. Among them was the ancestral home of the Wager family, which had produced several men prominent in state and national affairs, including Daniel E. Wager, prominent Rome jurist and historian, and General Henry Wager Halleck, chief of staff for the Union forces in the early years of the Civil War.

Delta folks saw the necessity for the dam, but they did not take kindly to moving from homes they had built and inhabited for a century. Albert Wadsworth was living in a house raised by his grandfather. The brick used had been manufactured in the dooryard. An aged widow complained, "I have been living in this house forty years and I did not suppose we would ever have to leave it." "I would about as soon die as be driven from this house," wailed another Delta resident.

Delta folks accepted the inevitable, but they resented the abrupt manner used by the state in dealing with them. One man receivd a notice on April 1, 1909, telling him of the proposed seizure of his land; on April 17 he got a second notice ordering him to be out by May 1. Furthermore, the state did not propose to pay right away, with the result that the evacuated citizens had to re-establish themselves elsewhere on their own money.

The state went right ahead despite many protests and a few suits.

The buildings were razed, the bodies in the cemetery removed, the dam built. Today the old village of Delta lies at the bottom of the reservoir.

Hinckley took the matter of evacuation more philosophically. The position of the dam would not affect the main part of the village. Only two industries would be ruined by the lake which would extend nine miles up the West Canada Creek. Up Northwood way, Bill Finch, who had run a wood alcohol plant for 27 years and had put up a store, a church and some houses, got the state to move all his buildings except the factory to higher ground, and went into the real estate business by selling camp sites to city slickers. Dan McCarthy, whose cheese factory had sent farmers across the Twin Rocks bridge in droves, paid his last check and closed up shop. The farmers tucked his checks in old socks and did not cash them for years: they knew Dan kept a bank balance large enough to cover such emergencies.

The inhabitants of Little Italy and Little Brooklyn, two settlements wandering along on opposite sides of the creek above Hinckley, picked up their belongings and their state checks and either moved into Hinckley or left for parts unknown, as did several farmers who were happy to be paid off for leaving land they had tried to farm unsuccessfully. Hinckley continued to roar for a decade after the land had been flooded, but the collapse of the Trenton Falls Lumber Company and the Hinckley Fibre Company brought an end to industrial activity.

Today Delta and Hinckley lakes are beauty spots visited by countless fishermen and campers. Except for brief periods of low water, they can rival natural lakes in beauty, and Hinckley Lake, with its backdrop of mountains, trees and sky, often evokes gasps of admiration from visitors seeing it for the first time.

The lakes have served their twin purpose; the barge canal is always sure of a constant supply of water; the Mohawk Valley cities and towns no longer suffer from floods. And, above all, the lakes have added to the beauty of the Adirondack foothills and have provided recreation for countless city families.

THE BATTLE OF BOONVILLE

As dawn broke over Boonville on Tuesday, August 1, 1933, farmers gathered along the highways leading to the village, their purpose being to dissuade other farmers from delivering cans of whole milk to the three plants in Boonville. The men were participating in a state-wide strike for better milk prices. They realized that they were breaking the law by holding up trucks and they were aware that forty state troopers had registered at the Hulbert House to keep law and order.

The summer of 1933 saw the worst drought in over fifteen years. Pastures dried up and water had to be hauled for the cows. When the patience of the farmers had been stretched to the breaking point, Albert Woodhead proclaimed from his Rochester headquarters that unless the farmers got a flat 45 per cent of the retail price of milk a state-wide strike would be called for August 1.

So, at dawn of that fateful day, farmers all over the state were taking up positions on highways leading to milk plants, hoping to stop other farmers from delivering milk. They planned no violence and for the most part were a pleasantly determined crowd of men who joked back and forth with curiosity-seekers who had come to see the fun.

About six-thirty the troopers dispersed a crowd at the junction of the roads to Alder Creek and Hawkinsville. The farmers came back, bringing with them many spectators. An hour later a truck was stopped. The strikers took off four cans of milk, placed them at the side of the road and helped themselves to drinks.

A group had congregated near a milk plant at the southern end of the village. A large body of state troopers emerged from the plant, took a good look at the crowd, and went back inside. They reappeared in a few minutes, wearing steel helmets and carrying riot stricks, gas bombs, gas masks and semi-machine guns. Without warning, they charged into the crowd and wielded their sticks on striker and bystander alike. Soon all was confusion. A gas bomb thrown by a trooper struck a man and inflicted a nasty gash in his side. It also sprayed him from head to foot with greenish-yellow gas. A youngster was pushed against a barbed wire fence and given a thorough going over with sticks. Men with bloodied heads ran for shelter, while women shrieked with fear.

The troopers marched in military array toward the gathering near the Hawkinsville road. The strikers retired to the sides of the highway, but the troopers charged into them, brandishing sticks and yelling for them to disperse. They even chased men into the fields, knocked them down and beat them while they lay defenseless on the ground.

So it went all over the Adirondack foothills. Two men were beaten and their car smashed in Remsen. Similar reports came all the way from Holland Patent to Constableville.

Boonville flew into an uproar. Two thousand people gathered that evening before the Hulbert House, to which place Major John A. Warner, head of the state police, had been summoned by telephone. Here he held a conference with Captain McGrath of the police unit at Boonville, members of the village board and representatives of the striking farmers. In the meanwhile, Dr. C. R. Barlett and other Boonville physicians were ministering to seventeen men who had been injured, some of them severely, and prominent Boonville citizens were preparing to take the matter up with Governor Herbert H. Lehman.

Major Warner issued a report that the troopers had collected countless sticks and clubs from the strikers. He also refuted the charge that his men had used brutality.

Garry Willard of the *Boonville Herald* struck back in an editorial: "For all the investigating Major Warner did, he might better have stayed away from Boonville. He but added fuel to the fires of local indignation by his failure to probe more deeply into the situation. His methods were decidedly unfair. They showed little regard for the wrought up feeling and rights of the people. If his methods are samples of how his department works in upholding the authority of the law, then it is high time something was done to correct it."

Willard and a delegation went to see Governor Lehman, who received them courteously but did not commit himself.

In October, when the price of milk had slid to $1.70 per 100 pounds, the Grand Jury refused to return any indictments. It ruled that the assembly of strikers was unlawful and should have dispersed when ordered to do so by officers of the law. It admitted that the officers may have used unseeming force in carrying out their duties and censured them for so doing.

The Battle of Boonville resulted in a legal stalemate, but resentment against state troopers lingered on for years.

THE LAST LOG DRIVE

For over a century, logs were driven each spring down the swift waters of the West Canada Creek and the Moose and Black Rivers to the lumbering villages of Hinckley, Lyons Falls and Forestport. Drives down these uncontrolled streams were hazardous affairs at best and the river boss, like a general before a battle, had to "high-spot" the drive by picking the exact time when the water level and the wind conditions were right for the logs to be run. Any miscalculation would result in dangerous riding for the riverjacks, and many an intrepid jack lost his life by attempting a run of water too swollen for navigation.

Logs could be "ornery critters" that headed toward a "backsny" or pocket near shore and had to be coaxed into the current through skillful shoves of peavey and pike pole. Riverjacks, wearing stout boots studded on the soles and heels with needle-pointed projections known officially as calks and colloquially as "corks," danced from log to log, prodding them with peaveys; or rode thirteen-footers down a stretch of "white water" with the skill and grace of circus acrobats. These riverjacks were the glamor boys of the streams, and stories of their exploits make up a considerable body of Adirondack foothills folklore. Old-timers still refer affectionately to Sol Carnahan or other departed riverjacks as "catty" or a "bubble-walker."

Despite the dexterity of the riverjacks, logs would act "ornery" and pile up in what were known as "jams." Even on well-organized drives, where skilled jacks were stationed at bends in the streams, a few logs would get tangled and before long the whole drive descended upon them, with the result that logs got piled up like "match sticks," completely blocking passage down the river. At such times the jacks needed the expert assistance of the "jam blower," who could discover the log or logs which were causing the trouble and "pull the plug," either with or without the use of dynamite. Loosening a jam often sent logs in all directions and many a jack "washed his clothes" in the cold stream and some lost their lives by being crushed or drowned.

Drives on the Moose River continued until 1947, when the dam at McKeever went out during the spring drive. Twenty hours of heavy rain raised the waters of the river to seven feet above normal. The old stone and crib-work dam, owned by the Gould Paper Company, could not stand the strain of logs and water. News that thousands of logs were hurtling down the Moose River alarmed the people of Lyons Falls, who hoped that something would stop the logs before they knocked down the famous three-way bridge.

Drives had been carried on for over a century without undue publicity. Most tales of riverjack bravery had come from the lips of friends who had witnessed their exploits and who probably had embroidered them somewhat. This last drive was to bring to the Moose River hundreds of spectators who had learned of the event through radio and the newspapers. Lyonsdale, a few miles above Lyons Falls, became a magnet to countless automobiles. The bridge across the river made a splendid grandstand. City-slickers saw for the first time riverjacks darting from log to log, trying desperately to hold back the roaring stampede of thirteen-footers and ease them into Ager's Bay, the one natural set-back between the falls at Lyonsdale and the log boom at Lyons Falls. This boom, consisting of concrete piers, was designed for an emergency, but this stampede exceeded all expectations, and the engineers were not too confident that it would confine all the logs which were racing madly down the river.

Logs came hurtling through so fast that the men could not control them. They piled up like jackstraws above the falls and their creaking and groaning could be heard through the shouts of the riverjacks and the roar of the falls. It became obvious that somebody would have to "pull the plug" and get the logs rolling before the whole mass let loose and tumbled down the river.

A dull roar sounded through the valley and logs were thrown high into the air from the force of the explosion the dynamite had germinated. Jacks worked feverishly to guide loose logs down the stream. They played a game of jack-straws with peaveys, loosening a log here and a log there, until the jam gave way. News came up the river that boom at Lyons Falls was holding. The riverjacks, working their last operation before a huge audience, had outdone themselves. Few logs had been lost and nothing had been destroyed.

Logs are no longer run down the foothills rivers. They are now hauled to the mills by heavily-laden trucks which sway back and forth under their loads, throwing fear into the hearts of passing motorists.

SOFTBALL MADNESS

Motorists passing through Barneveld on August 11, 1948, had to pick their way through parked cars and dodge men, women and children who were dashing toward their destination, the lighted softball field behind Moore's Hotel, where the local heroes, the Trenton Firemen, were to do battle with their arch-rivals, the Prospect Firemen, for the championship of the Firemen's League.

This lighted field had been installed about eight years earlier, at a time when baseball players scoffed at pitchers who "threw a ball like a girl." It was a curious diamond, tucked in between the hotel, the firehouse and a high embankment. The infield was several feet too narrow, and ground rules almost made an interpreter necessary, but it served the purpose of popularizing night softball in the foothills.

Veterans returning from World War II were prime movers in getting the Firemen's League organized in 1946. Charter members were Holland Patent, Poland, Prospect, Remsen, Stittville and Trenton. Prospect, the most die-hard baseball village, put up lights in that year, and Remsen and Holland Patent followed suit in 1948.

That was the summer in which night softball reached the stage of madness. Prospect, boasting a strong team, got off to a flying start and won its first ten games. "Beat Prospect" became the league slogan, and even at its home games the front-running team found the majority of the spectators in the enemy's corner. Trenton, also a powerful outfit, had lost two games when it come to Prospect in a do-or-die mood on August 2nd. The home team was nicely ahead when Trenton came up with seven runs in the sixth inning to send their team ahead to stay. A few days later, Prospect, which had won the Oneida County championship and had represented the Utica District at the State Tournament, got dumped by Newport, thus throwing them into a flat-footed tie with Trenton for first place.

By this time, the fans in the villages talked nothing but softball, and a few arguments at bars were broken up short of fisticuffs. Even the farmers forgot about milk prices in order to replay games across fences with their neighbors.

All was going well until Stittville and Holland Patent, who did not love each other as brothers, met in a twilight contest at Stittville.

147

The late innings were played in semi-darkness. Stittville had a runner on first base when a ball was hit through the Holland Patent infield. The visitors claimed that the Stittville base runner had been hit by the batted ball and was out. The Stittville umpire failed to agree and Holland Patent lost the game.

Their protest was aired for three consecutive evenings at the Butterfield House in Holland Patent. The meeting was an example of democracy at its best or at its worst. Holland Patent had not entered its protest at the time the play took place, thus technically invalidating its legality, but emotion seemed more important than intelligence at this meeting. At midnight of the third session, a vote of the managers was taken, and Holland Patent lost its protest. The three managers who had voted against Holland Patent were known for the rest of the season as "the three snakes in the grass."

Despite this unpleasantry, the villagers and farmers poured into Barneveld on August 11th. To hold the crowd, all the bleachers from the other fields were set up behind Moore's Hotel. They failed to accommodate the 1,600 spectators, who swarmed along the sidelines, covered the bank in the outfield, and even sat on the firehouse roof.

Prospect got off to a 9-2 lead, but Trenton still had a spark left. They pounded out four runs in the sixth inning, while the crowd split its collective throat with roars of approval. This rally proved to be a final gesture, for the Prospect pitcher bore down and retired the side in the last inning, and Prospect went home with the bacon, plus a considerable sum in side bets.

This game probably represented the high point for night softball in the foothills. The league had two more good years, but interest fell off and it collapsed after the season of 1953. Prospect still carries on with an expert team and an invitational tournament which attracts the best teams in the Mohawk Valley and brings over a thousand people to see the finals each Labor Day. A boys' league, organized in 1956, may keep the light poles on the other fields from becoming ghostly reminders of that summer when softball reached a stage of madness in the foothills.

THE FOOTHILLS TODAY

Probably the two best vantage points from which to enjoy the full sweep of the Adirondack foothills are Starr Hill, immediately above the Steuben memorial outside Remsen, and Buck Hill, several miles to the northwest. Starr Hill, named after a Revolutionary War veteran and not a celestial body, dominates the landscape and is said to be the highest point' in Oneida County. It overlooks the West Canada Valley, with its rolling farms and tree-laden villages. On clear days, Oneida Lake shimmers along the horizon. From Buck Hill, one can look down toward Western and Northwestern and follow the line of the old Black River Canal into Lake Delta.

The landscape has not changed appreciably since the horse and buggy days. Farms and woodlots still predominate. The most striking sign of progress is the network of hard roads which winds back and forth through the hills and valleys, indicating that the most remote farm is no longer isolated.

These roads are the result of two developments; the gasoline age and the centralization of schools. Powerful motors make child's play of hills which often taxed the sturdiest horse. Buses wind through the hills, carrying children to and from centralized schools in Remsen,· Forestport, Holland Patent and Boonville.

Homes all through the foothills boast antennae on their roofs, for the cities have been brought to the farms and villages through a vast network of radio and television. The foothills farmer, who now gets his morning newspaper delivered by rural free delivery, finds that the two mechanical devices keep him informed ahead of the printed word; and they also bring him plays, motion pictures and sporting events. Farm kitchens are filled with modern conveniences and barns contain tractors, milking machines and other devices for speeding up and alleviating the arduous labor of the farmer.

He still gripes, however, for the vicious circle of low milk prices and the high cost of maintenance lies uppermost in his mind, and he often wonders if he will be able to make the next payment on his automobile or television set.

The villages have changed more than have the farms. Mills along creeks no longer make meal and flour. General stores do not stock everything from a toothpick to a suit of clothes. Streams of automobiles carry workers from the villages to the Griffiss Air Base and to manufacturing plants in Utica and Rome. These men do not move their families to the city, for they feel that with the excellent schooling provided and the healthy atmosphere of the hills, their children will be happier and make more progress than they would make in a city.

Foothills villages have made giant strides in providing activities for youngsters. Boonville, a pioneer in the field of organized recreation, has excellent play fields and a swimming pool. Memorial fields serve as playgrounds for Holland Patent, Barneveld, Remsen and Prospect. Further north, the Leydens and Lyons Falls have actively supported programs for children.

Tremendous gains have been made in the matter of fire protection. The powerful pumpers one sees at the various field days are far cries from the "Old Tub" of the Boonville Cataract Boys. Volunteer fire companies still maintain their individuality, but they have learned to join together under a mutual aid system, with the result that firemen receive specialized training and act co-operatively in fighting big fires.

The television set has brought folks back into the home after years of chasing hither and yon in fast automobiles, but the old art of conversation seems to have gone and it is a rare occasion when farmers invite friends in for a pop-corn bee or a sugar-off.

Old timers look back through rosy-colored glasses and claim that the world has gone to the devil, but few of them would replace modern civilization for the inconveniences of the nineteenth century. The Adirondack foothills have truly come of age, and we who live amidst these beautiful and healthy surroundings are well aware of the fact.